LETTERS FOR THE AGES

LETTERS FOR THE AGES

The Private and Personal Letters of Sir Winston Churchill

Edited by James Drake and Allen Packwood

BLOOMSBURY CONTINUUM
LONDON · OXFORD · NEW YORK · NEW DELHI · SYDNEY

BLOOMSBURY CONTINUUM
Bloomsbury Publishing Plc
50 Bedford Square, London, WC1B 3DP, UK
29 Earlsfort Terrace, Dublin 2, Ireland

BLOOMSBURY, BLOOMSBURY CONTINUUM and the Diana logo are trademarks
of Bloomsbury Publishing Plc

First published in Great Britain 2023

For legal purposes the Acknowledgements on p. xiv constitute an extension
of this copyright page

A catalogue record for this book is available from the British Library

Library of Congress Cataloguing-in-Publication data has been applied for

ISBN: HB: 978-1-3994-0817-2; eBook: 978-1-3994-0813-4; ePDF: 978-1-3994-0814-1

2 4 6 8 10 9 7 5 3 1

Typeset by Deanta Global Publishing Services, Chennai, India
Printed and bound in Great Britain by CPI Group (UK) Ltd, Croydon CR0 4YY

To find out more about our authors and books visit www.bloomsbury.com
and sign up for our newsletters

CONTENTS

Acknowledgements   xiv

Editorial Conventions   xv

Preface   xvi
    Lord (Michael) Dobbs

INTRODUCTION: THE CHURCHILL LETTERS   xvii
    Allen Packwood and James Drake

CHAPTER ONE: THE EARLY YEARS (1883–94)   1

'I hope you will come and see me soon'   1
    1: from Winston to his mother, Lady Randolph Churchill,
    17 June 1883

'My dear Oom'   4
    2: from Winston to Mrs Everest, October 1884

'You must be happy without me'   6
    3: from Winston to Lady Randolph, 21 January 1885

'I know that you are very busy indeed'   7
    4: from Winston to his father, Lord Randolph Churchill,
    5 April 1885

'I feel as if I could cry at every thing'   9
    5: from Winston to Mrs Everest, 1886

'I can think of nothing else but the Jubilee'   10
    6: from Winston to Lady Randolph, 11 June 1887
    7: from the same, 12 June 1887

'It is that thoughtlessness of yours which is your greatest enemy'   14
    8: from Lady Randolph to her son, Winston, 12 June 1890
    9: from Winston to Lady Randolph, 19 June 1890

'Capital girl – good old hero – splendid villain'   18
    10: from Winston to Lady Randolph, 19 September 1890

'I will venture to further ventilate my grievances'   21
    11: from Winston writing as 'De Profundis' to the editor of
    The Harrovian, *November 1891*

'A mere social wastrel'   22
    12: from Lady Randolph to Winston, 7 August 1893
    13: from Lord Randolph to Winston, 9 August 1893
    14: from Winston to Lady Randolph, 17 September 1893

'Papa wrote me a long letter about the watch and seems to be very cross'   28
    15: from Lord Randolph to Winston, 21 April 1894
    16: from Winston to Lady Randolph, 24 April 1894

'I had never realised how ill Papa had been'   31
    17: from Winston to Lady Randolph, 2 November 1894

CHAPTER TWO: THOUGHTS AND ADVENTURES (1895–99)   34

'It is a fine game to play – the game of politics'   34
    1: from Winston to Lady Randolph, 16 August 1895

'What an extraordinary people the Americans are'   36
    2: from Winston to his brother, Jack Churchill, 15 November 1895

'Burn this Jack without showing to anyone'   39
    3: from Winston to the Reverend James Welldon, Headteacher
    at Harrow, 16 December 1896 (draft)

'To beat my sword into a paper cutter' 42
   4: from Winston to Lady Randolph, 23 December 1896

'You cannot but feel ashamed of yourself' 44
   5: from Lady Randolph to Winston, 26 February 1897

'I am a Liberal in all but name' 47
   6: from Winston to Lady Randolph, 6 April 1897

'I have faith in my star' 51
   7: from Winston to Lady Randolph, 5 September 1897
   8: from the same, 19 September 1897

'It is not so much a question of brains as of
character & originality' 55
   9: from Winston to Lady Randolph, 26 January 1898
   10: from the same, 15 July 1898

'We both know what is good – and we both like to
have it' 60
   11: from Winston to Lady Randolph, 28 January 1898

'All this in 120 seconds' 62
   12: from Winston to Colonel Sir Ian Hamilton,
     16 September 1898

'I do not consider that your Government was
justified in holding me' 67
   13: from Winston to Louis de Souza, 11 December 1899

CHAPTER THREE: PUTTING DOWN ROOTS
(1900–1914) 70

'My place is here' 70
   1: from Winston to Pamela Plowden, 28 January 1900
   (James Drake Collection)

'I do not feel I would be breaking up our home'   75
    2: from Lady Randolph to Winston, 26 May 1900

'I hate the Tory party – their men, their words, &
  their methods'   77
    3: from Winston to Hugh Cecil, 24 October 1903 (draft)

'A frank & clear-eyed friendship'   80
    4: from Winston to Clementine Hozier, 16 April 1908
    5: from the same, 27 April 1908

'I do not love & will never love any woman in the
  world but you'   84
    6: from Winston to Clementine, 10 November 1909

'We are getting into v[er]y gr[ea]t peril over Female
  Suffrage'   86
    7: from Winston to Alexander Murray, 18 December 1911

'The strict observance of the great traditions of the
  sea towards women & children reflects nothing
  but honour upon our civilisation'   89
    8: from Winston to Clementine, 18 April 1912

'I will not fly any more'   91
    9: from Winston to Clementine, 6 June 1914

CHAPTER FOUR: THE WORLD CRISIS (1914–18)   94

'Everything trends towards catastrophe and
  collapse'   94
    1: from Winston to Clementine, 28 July 1914
    2: from the same, 31 July 1914

'The caterpillar system would enable trenches to be
  crossed quite easily'   100
    3: from Winston to Herbert Asquith, 5 January 1915

'D-mn the Dardanelles! They'll be our grave!'   102
    4: from Admiral Fisher to Winston, 5 April 1915
    5: from Winston to Admiral Fisher, 8 April 1915

'The Dardanelles has run on like a Greek tragedy'   106
    6: from Winston to Admiral Sir John Jellicoe, 1 June 1915

'I am a spirit confident of my rights'   108
    7: from Winston to Clementine, 17 July 1915

'I have found happiness & content such as I have
    not known for many months'   111
    8: from Winston to Clementine, 23 November 1915
    9: from the same, 25 November 1915

'The cruel politics of today'   115
    10: from Winston to Clementine, 10 January 1916
    11: from the same, 13 January 1916

'The War is a terrible searcher of character'   119
    12: from Clementine to Winston, 16 March 1916
    13: from the same, 24 March 1916

'The party of the future might be formed'   124
    14: from Winston to Frederick (F. E.) Smith, 6 April 1916
    15: from the same, 8 April 1916

'Death seems as commonplace & as little alarming
    as the undertaker'   127
    16: from Winston to Clementine, 23 February 1918

CHAPTER FIVE: THE EMERGING STATESMAN
(1921–39)   131

'These last weeks have been cruel'   131
    1: from Winston to Lord Northcliffe, 1 July 1921

'I cannot stir a yard to defend myself'   **132**
  2: from Winston to J. C. Robertson, President of the Dundee
     Liberal Association, 27 October 1922

'No more champagne is to be bought'   **136**
  3: from Winston to Clementine, late summer 1926

**'A general strike is a challenge to the State, to the
Constitution and to the nation'**   **140**
  4: from Winston to Sir James Hawkey, 16 November 1926

'Most of … our lives are over now'   **142**
  5: from Winston to Hugo Baring, 8 February 1931

**'Germany is now the greatest armed power in
Europe'**   **145**
  6: from Winston to Clementine, 13 April 1935

**'Luckily I have plenty of things to do to keep me
from chewing the cud too much'**   **148**
  7: from Winston to Clementine, 30 December 1935

**'How melancholy that we have this helpless Baldwin
and his valets in absolute possession of all power!'**   **151**
  8: from Winston to Clementine, 15–17 January 1936

'A dozen bottles of sunshine'   **153**
  9: from Winston to Lord Horne of Slamannan, 27 January 1936

'This Spanish business cuts across my thoughts'   **154**
  10: from Winston to Anthony Eden, 7 August 1936

**'The combination of public and private stresses is
the hardest of all to endure'**   **156**
  11: from Winston to Stanley Baldwin, 5 December 1936

**'I thought y[our] remark singularly unkind,
offensive, & untrue'**   **159**
  12: from Winston to his son, Randolph Churchill,
     14 February 1938

'I am in no way responsible for what has happened'   161
    13: from Winston to Henry Page Croft, October or November
    1938 (draft)

'Can't we get at it?'   163
    14: from Winston to Neville Chamberlain, 30 August 1939
    (draft)
    15: from Winston to Sir Samuel Hoare, 8 October 1939
    16: from Winston to Lord Halifax, 1 November 1939

CHAPTER SIX: THE FINEST HOUR (1940–45)   169

'I am under no illusions about what lies ahead'   169
    1: from Winston to Neville Chamberlain, 10 May 1940

'This honour was deserved by your successful
execution of a most difficult task'   171
    2: from Winston to Vice-Admiral Sir Bertram Ramsay,
    17 June 1940

'There is a danger of your being generally disliked'   172
    3: from Clementine to Winston, 27 June 1940

'Never surrendering or scuttling her Fleet'   175
    4: from Winston to President Roosevelt, 31 August 1940

'It's a grand life, if we don't weaken'   176
    5: from Winston to Neville Chamberlain, 20 October 1940

'Sail on, O Ship of State'   179
    6: from President Roosevelt to Winston: 20 January 1941

'Now or never. "A nation once again"'   181
    7: from Winston to Éamon de Valera, 8 December 1941

'Burn this letter when you have read it'   182
    8: from Winston to President Roosevelt, 25 February 1942

'I do not want the lion at the moment'   184
    9: from Winston to the Duke of Devonshire, 13 February 1943

'A man who has to play an effective part in taking, with the highest responsibility, grave and terrible decisions of war may need the refreshment of adventure'   186
>   *10: from King George VI to Winston, 2 June 1944*
>   *11: from Winston to King George VI, 3 June 1944*

'Ever since 1907, I have in good times and bad times, been a sincere friend of France'   190
>   *12: from Winston to General Charles de Gaulle, 16 June 1944*

'Thus two-thirds of our forces are being mis-employed for American convenience, and the other third is under American Command'   192
>   *13: from Winston to Clementine, 17 August 1944*

'No more let us falter! From Malta to Yalta! Let nobody alter!'   195
>   *14: telegram from Winston to President Roosevelt, 1 January 1945*

'You may be sure I shall always endeavour to profit by your counsels'   197
>   *15: from Clement Attlee to Winston, 19 January 1945*
>   *16: from Winston to Attlee, 20 January 1945 (draft, not sent)*
>   *17: from Winston to Attlee, 22 January 1945*

CHAPTER SEVEN: AFTERMATH AND LEGACY (1945–64)   203

'Here is the rock of safety'   203
>   *1: from Winston to Ernest Bevin, 13 November 1945*

'It will be a great shock to the British nation to find themselves, all of a sudden, stripped of their Empire'   206
>   *2: from Winston to Clement Attlee, 1 May 1946 (draft)*

'I revived the ancient and glorious conception
   of a United Europe'   208
      3: from Winston to Léon Blum, 7 April 1948

'Intervention by a great state in the internal affairs
   of a small one is always questionable'   212
      4: from Winston to President Truman, 29 June 1949
      5: from President Truman to Winston, 2 July 1949

'For whoever wins there will be nothing but
   bitterness and strife'   215
      6: from Winston to Clementine, 19 January 1950

'I am writing to ask if you could consider giving
   me your kind services so that I may have some
   puppies by you'   218
      7: from Rufus of Chartwell to Jennifer of Post Green, March 1955

'To resign is not to retire'   219
      8: from Winston to President Eisenhower, April 1955 (draft)

'It will be an act of folly, on which our whole
   civilisation may founder'   221
      9: from Winston to President Eisenhower, 22 November 1956 (draft)

'Even a joke in my poor taste can be enjoyed'   224
      10: from Francis Crick to Winston, 12 October 1961

'I shall persevere'   226
      11: from Winston to Clementine, 18 June 1963

'I owe you what every Englishman, woman & child
   does – liberty itself'   228
      12: from Mary Soames to her father, Winston, 8 June 1964

About the Editors   231
Index   233

ACKNOWLEDGEMENTS

This book could not have been produced without the help and support of many people. We wish to acknowledge our gratitude to Her late Majesty Queen Elizabeth II for generously allowing the reproduction of the letter by her father. The support and encouragement of Mr Randolph Churchill and his late wife, the much-missed Catherine Churchill, was critical to the success of this project, as was that of Mr Laurence Geller, Chairman of the International Churchill Society, and his wife Jennie Churchill. We are grateful to Lord Dobbs for contributing his wonderful preface.

Quotes from the personal writings of Winston S. Churchill are reproduced with permission of Curtis Brown, London, on behalf of The Estate of Winston S. Churchill (© The Estate of Winston S. Churchill). Quotes from the personal writings of Lady Randolph Churchill, Lord Randolph Churchill and The Lady Soames DG DBE are reproduced with the permission of the Master, Fellows and Scholars of Churchill College Cambridge. Thanks are due to Michael Crick for permission to quote his father's letter. Images from the Broadwater Collection are reproduced with the permission of Curtis Brown, London. Images from the Baroness Spencer-Churchill papers are reproduced with the permission of Churchill College Cambridge. Thanks are due to Gordon Wise of Curtis Brown and Jessica Collins at Churchill Archives Centre. The work builds on the scholarship of the late Sir Martin Gilbert and previous generations of Churchill scholars. It would not exist without the inspiration of James Drake and Danny Al-Khafaji, Isabel Jacob and Helen Kwong at Of Lost Time.

EDITORIAL CONVENTIONS

While Churchill was undoubtedly a great writer, more often than not his letters were very lengthy and, therefore, unsuitable for printing in their entirety in a general edition of this nature. In the interest of publishing a readable and accessible book, some omissions have been made from the published version of the text; these cuts have been indicated by an ellipsis (...). For readers interested in viewing the letters in full, almost all of them can be viewed by appointment at the Churchill Archives Centre, Churchill College Cambridge (archives.chu.cam.ac.uk).

Text omitted by Churchill himself – often in unsent drafts where he crossed through sections to rewrite – has been published in the same fashion with a line through the centre. Additionally, Churchill frequently used abbreviations in his letters; in order to make his meanings obvious to the reader, most of these have an editorial explanation beside them in brackets.

PREFACE

I first stumbled across Winston Churchill as a teenager when I watched his funeral on a black-and-white television screen sitting beside my mother, whose cheeks were soaked with tears. Muffled drums beat out their sorrows, the cranes of London's docks lowered their heads in respect, and a fire was lit under my imagination that has lasted a lifetime.

I have spent most of those years since then either working in politics or re-imaging politics for the novel, stage or screen. I have both known and created characters who were villains or heroes and sometimes both, but none has captured me as much as Winston Churchill. When fact is stranger than fiction, we often fall back on the line 'you just could not make it up', but that phrase hardly does justice to the incredible life that you will encounter in these pages. He has been called a maverick, a buccaneer, an adventurer – and he was all those things – yet he also held most of the major offices of the British State and led us through the darkest hour of the twentieth century, through unimaginable horrors and onto sunlit uplands.

He could be egotistical, was eternally impatient, his opinions were loud and his faults manifest, but somewhere along the way he managed to save our world. He did that as much with words as with actions, and his mastery of language is apparent in his own letters. Through them we get glimpses of the real Winston – of the stubborn, wilful, rebellious schoolchild, the headstrong and ambitious soldier, the campaigning politician, the loving husband and father, and the resolute war leader. He was an exceedingly complex figure, as these letters reveal. They are not the artifice of today's media manipulators but the authentic Churchill, the unvarnished thoughts of a man in the most private moments of his extraordinary life.

I defy you not to be inspired.

Lord Dobbs

INTRODUCTION: THE CHURCHILL LETTERS

Winston Churchill has become an iconic figure but also a controversial one. He is celebrated for his warnings about fascism and communism, and for his inspirational leadership of Britain during the Second World War, but has also been attacked for his views on empire and race. With his famous bulldog scowl, spotted bow tie, ever-present cigar and eccentric clothing, he is one of the most instantly recognizable individuals of the modern era, and also one of the most widely quoted (and misquoted).

Churchill understood the power of words. He used his writing to sustain and complement his political career, producing over forty books and winning the Nobel Prize for Literature for his contribution to the written and spoken word. His speeches, especially his wartime broadcasts, are considered among the most powerful ever given in the English language.

This volume concentrates on his private words. It seeks to look behind the public figure and tell Churchill's story through a selection of his key letters, including some that he received from others and some that he drafted and then chose not to send. Churchill's official biography, started by his son Randolph and completed by Sir Martin Gilbert, runs to a colossal eight volumes with twenty-three additional companion volumes, and features a huge selection of his letters. This is not an attempt to replicate that work. Instead, it aims to provide an introduction and starting point: one that goes back to the sources (including some that are not featured elsewhere) in order to capture the drama, immediacy, storms, passions, challenges and triumphs of Churchill's remarkable roller-coaster career.

Churchill was neither god nor demon; he was human, with human emotions, frailties and ego. He was not always consistent; he was not always right. He held strong opinions and was often provocative. But he was both an active participant in and articulate observer of many of the most important episodes in our recent history and played an undeniable part in shaping the world we live in today. Here was a man who was born into the Victorian aristocracy, took part in a cavalry charge and lived through the reigns of six monarchs into the atomic age. He was active in British politics during six decades, and wrestled with most of the major social, economic, military and political challenges of his day. As Prime Minister during the Second World War he led Britain through its greatest crisis in modern times, pledging himself to a policy of waging war until victory, when that prospect seemed remote to many.

These letters take us into his world and allow us to follow the changes in his motivations and beliefs as he navigates his ninety years. They find him at his most honest and self-aware, often providing a unique private window on a life lived largely in public. It was certainly a life lived to the full.

Allen Packwood and James Drake

CHAPTER ONE

THE EARLY YEARS (1883–94)

'I HOPE YOU WILL COME AND SEE ME SOON'

Winston Leonard Spencer-Churchill made a characteristically dramatic entrance into this world when he was born prematurely at Blenheim Palace on 30 November 1874, probably one of the very few times in his life that he arrived early. Blenheim was the home of his grandfather, the Duke of Marlborough.

Winston's parents were Lord Randolph Churchill, a younger son of the Duke and therefore not eligible to succeed to the title, and Jennie Jerome, the beautiful Brooklyn-born daughter of the American entrepreneur Leonard Jerome from whom Winston took his middle name. They were a power couple. Randolph was a Member of Parliament and rising star within the Conservative Party and Jennie was an expert networker and high-society hostess.

Churchill's upbringing seems to have been a privileged but isolated one, with his younger brother Jack and his nanny Mrs Everest as his most constant companions. Time spent in Ireland, where his grandfather was Lord Lieutenant, and long stays at Blenheim instilled in him an early sense of history, privilege and power, but also fostered a lifelong spirit of independence and a stubborn streak that would clash with the strict regime of the Victorian boarding school.

Winston was sent away to St George's School in Ascot just before his eighth birthday. His letters home put a brave face on an unhappy period. The headmaster, Herbert Sneyd-Kynnersley, was a strict disciplinarian, infamous for caning his young pupils, and Churchill was a wilful and rebellious child, who was always late and whose conduct was described as 'extremely bad' and 'very naughty'. Churchill later wrote that, 'Where my reason, imagination or interest were not engaged, I would not or I could not learn.' This letter, written to his mother from the school, with its spelling mistakes for flower and aunts, its multiple kisses, his appeal for visits and the clear pleasure at the prospect of his 'comeinge [sic] home in a month' captures his loneliness. Surviving school was Churchill's first major challenge.

1: from Winston to his mother, Lady Randolph Churchill, 17 June 1883 (CHAR 28 / 13 / 17)

My dear Mamma,

I hope you will come and see me soon. Did Everest give you my flour [sic] I sent you. Give my love to my a[u]nts [sic] and tell not to forget to come down. I am comeinge [sic] home

<u>In a month</u>.

…W…I…T…H…

love & kisses

I

Remain

yours

loveing [sic]

Son

W. L. S. Churchill

XXX [etc.]

OO

kisses xooooxoo [etc.]

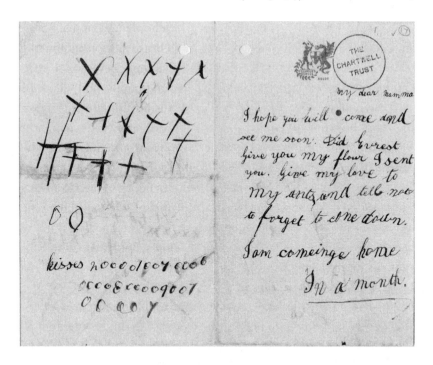

my dear mamma

I hope you will • come and see me soon. Did Everest give you my flour I sent you. Give my love to my anty and tell nore to forget to cme down.

I am comeinge home

In a month.

WINSTON, WEARING HIS SAILOR'S SUIT, C. 1881.

'MY DEAR OOM'

This scribbled note is a testament to Churchill's greatest childhood friendship. It is not written to a classmate, or even to his younger brother Jack, but rather to a little old lady, one Elizabeth Anne Everest, called 'Oom' by Churchill, short for 'Womany'; the name by which he knew his nanny.

The letter is not at all formal or scripted, as many of his earliest letters to his parents clearly were. It is written at speed, its purpose to convey the important news that the nine-year-old Winston has not been well to the one person guaranteed to respond with love, affection and care at such moments. As he later wrote, 'Mrs. Everest it was who looked after me and tended all my wants. It was to her I poured out my many troubles ...'

Little is known about Mrs Everest. She survives in one photograph, in the letters like this one between her and Winston, and in the affectionate and nostalgic portrait he paints of her in his memoir *My Early Life* where he calls her 'my dearest and most intimate friend'. Her influence on Winston was profound. She had been born at Chatham in Kent and her great love of that county undoubtedly inspired Churchill's desire to live there; an ambition that would be fulfilled in 1922 with the purchase of his home, Chartwell. She was intensely patriotic and anti-Catholic, instilling in her young charge low-church Protestant values that led him to support the established church from the outside (as he claimed, like a buttress) and grounding him in English hymns and the King James Bible from which he would later draw some of his most famous oratory. She took him on holiday to stay with her sister at Ventnor on the Isle of Wight where he learned how normal people lived, relishing the stories of prison mutinies and Zulu wars told to him by Mrs Everest's brother-in-law, a former prison warder. The reference to artillery relates to his toy soldier collection.

It was Mrs Everest who looked out for Winston and her advice was probably critical in getting him removed from St George's School, when his health deteriorated under its harsh regime, and sent to a more liberal establishment in Brighton.

2: from Winston to Mrs Everest, October 1884 (CHAR 28 / 13 / 44)

My dear Oom,

I have not been very well this week. I woke up one morning with a cr[o]upy cough. Mrs. Ottway kept me in bed all day and the next day she would not let me go out but I am all right now.

...

You must excuse this scribble as I wrote it in a hurry. I shall soon be looking for a visit from you so you must ask Mamma to let you come and see me with Jack.

Give my love to him and tell him he may have my little artillery. Now I must say goodbye as I am going to give Mamma a lecture for not writing to me.

With love and kisses, I remain yours affect[ionately]

Winston

kisses for you

xxxx [etc]

P.S I got 2 1 5 marks my frist [sic] <u>week</u> and my 2nd I got 2 8 5.

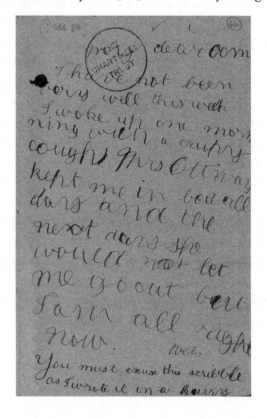

'YOU MUST BE HAPPY WITHOUT ME'

Much has been written about Lord and Lady Randolph Churchill
being distant parents, but it is also fair to say that Winston was not the
easiest child. There are plenty of indications that his behaviour could
be troublesome and in this letter to his mother he is damned by his
own admission that life at home for her 'must be heaven on earth'
now that he was back at school in Brighton. It followed a Christmas
holiday in which he had clearly provoked the screams and complaints
of his brother Jack. Churchill obviously had a temper. There was
a legend at St George's School that his response to a flogging had
been to seize the headmaster's straw hat and kick it to pieces. The
Brighton sea air and the small Brunswick Road school were supposed
to provide a healthier and more calming environment. The move was
made on the recommendation of Dr Robson Roose, the family doctor
mentioned in the letter, whose son Bertie was a pupil in Brighton.

Churchill was already aware that he was the son of a famous
father. Lord Randolph Churchill was a controversial figure, famous
for his cutting speeches. In January 1885, he was in the middle of

an extensive tour of India, the most important colony in the British Empire, preparing for the role of Secretary of State for India should the Conservatives gain power. He would assume the position in June and oversee the annexation of neighbouring Burma. The roots of Churchill's imperialism and his later opposition to Indian independence began with his admiration for his father and his determination to defend his legacy.

3: from Winston to Lady Randolph, 21 January 1885 (CHAR 28 / 13 / 47)

Jan 21st 1885
29 Brunswick Road

My dear Mamma,

I hope you are well. I am getting on pretty well. The Play is on the 11th of February 1885. You must be happy Without me, no screams from Jack or complaints.

It must be heaven upon earth. Will you try and find out for me what day Dr Rouse [sic] is going to take me to see Dr Woaks write and tell me. Will you tell me what day the mail goes to India, because I want to write to him. Now I must say Good-bye.

With Love and kisses
I remain
Your Loving son
Winston

'I KNOW THAT YOU ARE VERY BUSY INDEED'

Winston always sought his father's approval. In this letter he tries to engage Lord Randolph by referencing politics and giving examples of his father's popularity among the people of Brighton. Like William Gladstone, the Prime Minister and leader of the Liberal Party, Randolph was a national figure, instantly identifiable in contemporary cartoons by his immaculately groomed moustache. Churchill is shrewd enough to ask his father for autographs, knowing that these can give him status among his classmates and perhaps earn him some additional pocket money. He could not have imagined that his own signature would ultimately be worth a lot more.

Unfortunately, Churchill's interest in his father was not reciprocated. Just a few months later in October 1885, he would write to Lord Randolph again complaining that his father had visited Brighton without coming to see him. Winston had no choice but to excuse his parent, acknowledging that he knew Lord Randolph was 'very busy indeed'. He would have been disappointed had he known the truth. For it is clear from a letter sent by Randolph to Jennie that he had only travelled to the coast for 'a little fresh air' after nearly a fortnight in London. His relaxation simply did not include time for a meeting with his ten-year-old son.

Churchill's letter also makes reference to his riding: a pursuit that he had started in the grounds of Blenheim before going to school and that was to become his passion and vocation.

4: from Winston to his father, Lord Randolph Churchill, 5 April 1885 (CHAR 28 / 13 / 59)

29&30 Brunswick Rd.
April 5th 1885.

My darling Papa,

I hope you are quite well. The weather continues very fine though there has been a little rain lately. I have been out riding with a gentleman who thinks that Gladstone is a brute and thinks that "the one with the curly moustache ought to be Premier"[.] The driver of the Electric Railway said "that Lord R Churchill would be Prime Minister". Cricket has become the foremost thought now. Every body wants your autograph but I can only say I will try, and I should like you to sign your name in full at the end of your letter.

I only want a scribble as I know that you are very busy indeed. With love and kisses

I remain
Your loving son
Winston

'I FEEL AS IF I COULD CRY AT EVERYTHING'

Winston's constitution was clearly weaker than his character. He had been sent to Brighton because it was felt to be a better place for his fragile health and there are suggestions that he may have been asthmatic. In March 1886 he fell dangerously ill with pneumonia, developing an extremely high fever. Such was the severity of his condition that this time both his parents rushed to Brighton, though Dr Roose would not initially let them see him. For a few days his life hung in the balance. In an age before antibiotics there was little that Roose could do other than wait for the point of crisis, after which Winston would either recover or die. Interestingly, he was treated with alcohol, perhaps his first exposure to spirits, though as they were not necessarily given by mouth this is unlikely to have been an enjoyable experience. Churchill's later quip, that he had taken more out of alcohol than alcohol had taken out of him, may not have been true on this occasion!

His recovery was slow and this letter to his nanny seems likely to have been written during this difficult time. Once again, he is able to show his true feelings. This was not to be his last battle with pneumonia. It would threaten his life again during the Second World War.

Churchill's poor health may have been one of the reasons he was later sent to Harrow School rather than Eton, where Lord Randolph had been educated. Both were considered among the very best (and most expensive) British public schools, but Harrow enjoyed a position on a hill outside London where the air was felt to be more favourable. Harrow may also have been considered the slightly less academic choice. Winston was yet to reveal his full potential, though it is clear that he could do well when motivated.

5: from Winston to Mrs Everest, 1886 (CHAR 28/13/88)

[1886]

My dearest Oom,

I rec[eive]d your letter. I am feeling very weak, I feel as if I could cry at every thing.

I was all right, after you left, till just this evening.

With love & kisses
I remain
Yours affect[ionately]
Winston

A YOUNG VICTORIAN GENTLEMAN.

'I CAN THINK OF NOTHING ELSE BUT THE JUBILEE'

Churchill was certainly motivated in the summer of 1887. In what can be seen as perhaps his earliest political campaign, he bombarded his mother with letters from school in Brighton imploring her to allow him to return to London and attend the Golden Jubilee celebrations marking Queen Victoria's fifty years on the British throne. He was particularly determined to see 'Buffalow Bill'. The Wild West Show of William F. Cody, known as Buffalo Bill, was the hot ticket of the season, complete with animals, Native Americans, feats of marksmanship and re-enactments.

Winston worked hard in these letters to circumvent the opposition of his teacher, urging his mother to write on his behalf, and even providing her with a text, his suggested draft ending with her initials 'J.S.C' for Jennie Spencer-Churchill. And just in case there was any room for doubt about his wishes, he signed off with 'For Heaven's Sake Remember!!!' and added a doodle of a cannon firing.

29-30 Brunswick Road
Brighton
Sunday

My dear Mummy,

I hope you are as well as I am. I am writing this letter to back up my last, I hope you will not disappoint me. I can think of nothing else but Jubilee. Uncertainty is at all times perplexing write to me by return post please!!! I love you so much dear Mummy and I know you love me too much to disappoint me. Do write to tell me what you intend to do. I must come home, I feel I must. Write to Miss Thomson a letter after this principle

so — "My dear ———

Could you allow Winston to come up to London, on Saturday the 18th for the Jubilee. I should like him to see the procession very much, and I also promised him that he should come up for the Jubilee.

I remain
Yours
J.S.C...

I think that the above will hit its mark, anyhow you can try. I know you will be successful.

I am looking forward to seeing Buffalow Bill, yourself, Jack, Everest, and home.

I would sooner come home for

His determination and ingenuity seem to have paid off. We know that he attended the Jubilee because on his return (perhaps unsurprisingly) he had to write apologizing for his bad behaviour. It may well have been during the Jubilee festivities that he was taken by his uncle, John Leslie, to Barnum's circus, another famous American entertainment. Years later, speaking in the House of Commons in 1931, he would use the experience to attack the Labour Leader and British Prime Minister Ramsay MacDonald, stating:

I remember when I was a child being taken to the celebrated Barnum's circus, which contained an exhibition of freaks and monstrosities, but the exhibit on the programme which I most desired to see was the one described as 'The Boneless Wonder'. My parents judged that spectacle would be too revolting and demoralizing for my youthful eyes and I have waited fifty years to see 'The Boneless Wonder' sitting on the Treasury Bench.

6: from Winston to Lady Randolph, 11 June 1887 (CHAR 28/14/17)

My dear Mamma,

Mrs [sic] Thomson does'nt [sic] want me to go home for the Jubilee and because she says that I shall have no place in Westminster Abbey and so it is not worth going. Also that you will be very busy and unable to be with me much. Now you know that this is not the case. I want to see Buffalo Bill – the Play as you promised me. I shall be very disappointed,

Disappointed is not the word I shall be miserable, after you have promised me, and all, I shall never trust your promises again. But I know that Mummy loves her Winny much too much for that.

Write to Mrs [sic] Thomson and say that you have promised me and you want to have me home.

Jack entreats you daily I know to let me come and there are 7 weeks after the Jubilee before I come home. Don't disappoint me. If you write to Miss Thomson she will not resist you, I could come home on Saturday & stay till Wednesday, I have got a lot of things, pleasant and unpleasant to tell you.

Remember for my sake. I am quite well but in a ferment about coming home it would upset me entirely if you were to stop me.

Love & kisses

I remain

Yours as ever

Loving Son

(Remember)   Winny

7: from the same, 12 June 1887 (CHAR 28/14/18-19)

29-30 Brunswick Road
Brighton
Sunday

My dear Mamma,

I hope you are as well as I am. I am writing this letter to back up my last, I hope you will not disappoint me. I can think of nothing else but Jubilee. Uncertainty is at all times perplexing write to me by return post please!!! I love you so much dear Mummy and I know you love me too much to disappoint me. Do write to tell me what you intend to do. I must come home, I feel I must. Write to Miss Thomson a letter after this principle

So:- "My dear ——

Could you allow Winston to come up to London, on Saturday the 18th for the Jubilee. I should like him to see the procession very much, and I also promised him that he should come up for the Jubilee.

I remain

Yours ———

J.S.C."

I think that the above will hit its mark, anyhow you can try. I know you will be successful.

I am looking forward to seeing Buffalow [sic] Bill, yourself, Jack, Everest, and <u>home</u>.

   ...

Please, as you love me, do as I have begged you.

Love to all

I remain as ever

Your loving son

Winny

<u>For Heaven's sake Remember!!!</u>

'IT IS THAT THOUGHTLESSNESS OF YOURS WHICH IS YOUR GREATEST ENEMY'

Churchill arrived at Harrow School in April 1888, aged thirteen. It must have been quite a shock, given the small size of the schools that he had previously attended (picture perhaps Harry Potter's first arrival at Hogwarts).

Unfortunately, the new surroundings did not generate a new approach. At the end of his first term, his House Master, Mr Davidson, wrote to his mother, complaining that, 'I do not think, nor does Mr Somervell, that he is any way wilfully troublesome; but his forgetfulness, carelessness, unpunctuality, and irregularity in every way, have really been so serious, that I write to ask you, when he is at home to speak very gravely to him on the subject.' He warns her that, 'Winston, I am sorry to say, has, if anything, got worse as the term passed. Constantly late for school, losing his books, and papers and various other things into which I need not enter – he is so regular in his irregularity that I really don't know what to do ...' He was soon placed on 'reports', meaning that his work was being closely monitored.

His behaviour could certainly get him into trouble. One of his early actions at Harrow was to push a small boy into the school swimming lake. It turned out to be the older Leo Amery. The two later both became politicians and Amery served as a minister in Churchill's wartime government.

He continued to be the recipient of further bad school reports, prompting his mother to write a perceptive letter in June 1890 in which she recognizes that her fifteen-year-old son's work is an insult to his intelligence and that he lacks method, determination and planning. In his reply, Churchill admits his own laziness and pledges to try harder. It was a promise he struggled to keep. In May 1891 the sixteen-year-old Winston got into what he called a 'deuce of a row'. In a letter to his father he had to admit how he and some friends 'discovered the ruins of a large factory, into which we climbed. Everything was in ruin and decay but some windows yet remained unbroken; we facilitated the progress of time with regard to these'. Unfortunately for the boys, they were also spotted by the watchman, who reported them to the Harrow headmaster, who then had them caned.

8: from Lady Randolph to her son, Winston, 12 June 1890 (CHAR 1/8/9-11)

Thursday 12th [June 1890]

Dearest Winston,

I am sending this by Everest, who is going to see how you are getting on – I would go down to you – but I have so many things to arrange about the Ascot party next week that I can't manage it – I have much to say to you, I'm afraid not of a pleasant nature. You know darling how I hate to find fault with you, but I can't help myself this time

. . .

Your report which I enclose is as you will see a <u>very</u> bad one – you work in such a fitful inharmonious way, that you are bound to come out last – look at your place in the form! Y[ou]r father & I are both more disappointed than one can say, that you are not able to go up for y[ou]r Preliminary Exam: I daresay you have a 1000 excuses for not doing so – but there the fact remains! If only you had a better place in your form, & were a little more methodical, I would <u>try</u> & find an excuse for you. Dearest Winston you make me very unhappy – I had built up such hopes about you and felt so proud of you – & now all is gone. My only consolation is that your conduct is good, & that you are an affectionate son – but your work is an insult to your intelligence. If you would only trace out a plan of action for yourself, & carry it out & be <u>determined</u> to do so – I am sure you could accomplish anything you wished. It is that thoughtlessness of yours which is your greatest enemy ... There is Jack on the other hand, who comes out as the head of his class every week.

. . .

Your loving but distressed Mother
JSC

HARROW, c. 1888.

9: from Winston to Lady Randolph, 19 June 1890 (CHAR 28 / 18 / 38-40)

[19 June 1890]

My darling Mummy,

... I will not try to excuse myself for not working hard, because I know that what with one thing and another I have been rather lazy. Consequently when the month ended the crash came I got a bad report & got put on reports etc. etc. That is more than 3 weeks ago, and in the coming month I am <u>bound</u> to get a good report as I have had to take daily reports to Mr Davidson twice a week and they have been very good on the whole.

...

My own Mummy I can tell you your letter cut me up very much. Still there is plenty of time to the end of term and I will do my <u>very best</u> in what remains. I wanted to go in for my Preliminary & I will explain the whole thing to you.

If in your Examination you succeed in passing any 3 of the 8 subjects you need only compete in those you failed in. Now I knew that if I worked at

1 Geography
2 French
3 & English Dictation & Composition

I should pass in all these.

I knew that work however hard at Mathematics I could not pass in that. All other boys going in were taught those things & I was not, so they said it was useless.

Good Bye my own
With love I remain
Your own
Winston S. Churchill

'CAPITAL GIRL – GOOD OLD HERO – SPLENDID VILLAIN'

Yet it was not all bad news and teenage troublemaking. Winston's early letters are also revealing of his love of drama and the stage, of theatre and music hall. In this letter to his mother, the fifteen-year-old Churchill writes from Harrow describing a night out in London at the Adelphi watching *The English Rose*; a typical melodrama of the time set in Ireland where the young Irish hero is in love with the daughter of an English landowner but finds himself falsely framed for her father's murder by the villainous land agent. All comes well in the end. Churchill describes it in the language of the time as a 'ripping piece' with 'capital songs', 'Capital girl – good old hero – splendid villain'.

The songs and scripts of Churchill's youth remained with him and he would often recite them in later life. He relished the joyfulness and wordplay in the operettas of Gilbert and Sullivan. One of his favourite toys was a miniature theatre and his early letters often mention school productions. The need to be centre stage and the love of performance is another strand of his character that starts to develop in these formative early years.

He clearly had an artistic streak to his nature, which can also be seen in the drawing adorning the top of this letter. It shows him in his school uniform, presumably waiting at the railway station for the train that would take him back to Harrow. As we will see, Churchill famously took up painting in later life, but the talent was clearly there if largely latent – something that was perhaps true of his schoolwork more generally.

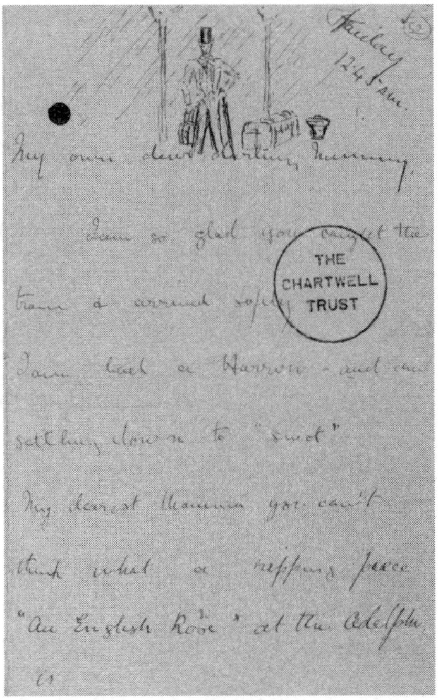

Friday 12.45 am.

My own dear darling Mummy,

I am so glad you caught the train & arrived safely. I am back at Harrow - and am settling down to "swot".

My dearest Mamma you can't think what a ripping piece "An English Rose" at the Adelphi is

THE CHARTWELL TRUST

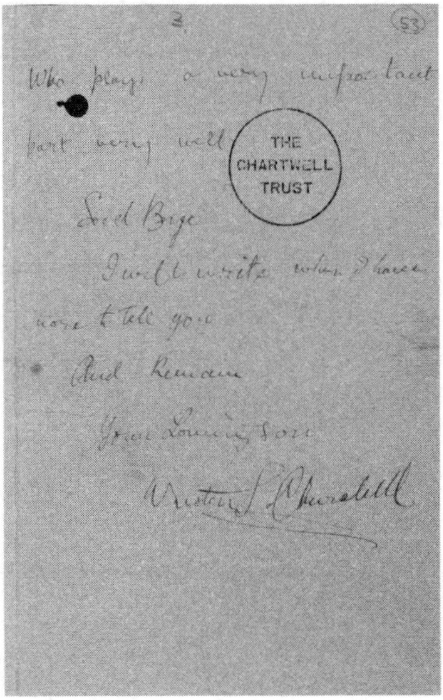

3

53

Who plays a very unfortunate part very well.

Good Bye

I will write when I have more to tell you

And Remain

Your Loving Son

Winston S Churchill

THE CHARTWELL TRUST

10: from Winston to Lady Randolph, 19 September 1890 (CHAR 28/17/52-53)

[19 Sept. 1890]
Friday
12.45 AM
My own dear, darling mummy,
I am so glad you caught the train & arrived safely.
I am back at Harrow – and am settling down to "swot".
My dearest Mamma you can't think what a ripping piece "An English Rose" at the Adelphi, is.
Well acted – well put on – excellently carried out – beautiful scenery – capital songs.

...

Capital girl – good old hero – splendid villain – Enchanting horse called 'Bally (Heaven knows what)' a very good sergeant of Constabulary who plays a very important part very well.
Good Bye
I will write when I have more to tell you
And Remain
Your Loving Son
Winston S. Churchill

JACK, LADY RANDOLPH AND WINSTON CHURCHILL, 1889.

'I WILL VENTURE TO FURTHER VENTILATE MY GRIEVANCES'

De Profundis, meaning 'from the depths', is used here by Winston as a pseudonym to hide his true identity. This is a letter from the depths of the school to the editor of Harrow's weekly newspaper criticizing the state of some of the classrooms, in some of which 'the wind of heaven has free access from every quarter'.

Written around the time of Churchill's seventeenth birthday, it shows an emerging mastery of English and a more mature writing style. The language is deliberately ironic and cynical. It marks one of Churchill's first forays into the world of journalism, a profession he would master over the course of the next decade. Churchill later credited his excellence in English to the fact that at Harrow he was not considered bright enough to progress quickly to learning Greek or Latin, so that Mr Somervell 'was charged with the duty of teaching the stupidest boys the most disregarded thing – namely, to write mere English'. As Churchill acknowledged, Somervell did this very well. In Churchill's case, it may also have been in the genes. His father was a famous orator and his mother wrote plays and articles and would go on to edit a short-lived literary journal called *The Anglo-Saxon Review*.

Winston's letter also reveals a continuing streak of anti-authoritarianism. But while he was still not prepared to conform to school ways, he had perhaps come to realize that the pen was an effective way of voicing discontent, more effective perhaps than trampling the headmaster's hat. He had begun to find his voice. But what was his career to be?

11: from Winston writing as 'De Profundis' to the editor of The Harrovian, *November 1891 (CHAR 1/3/4)*

Dear Sirs,

Since you so kindly printed my last letter, I will venture to further 'ventilate my grievances'. I will not act without precedent. In a number published two or three terms ago, you sanctioned a discussion on the advantages and defects of the Harrow "Hat". Therefore I make my complaint.

The Class rooms provided for several forms are very bad. In some the light is meagrely doled out as in the Old Music Room, the Towers of the New Speech Room and Mr Welsford's Room. In others as the 'cock-loft' the wind of Heaven has free access from every quarter. Something ought to be done. Either the number of the school should not exceed the number for whom proper accommodation can be provided or new Class Rooms should be built. Since that conspicuous, though unsightly edifice, the Music Schools was erected with so much ease I would respectfully suggest the latter alternative.

Yours etc.

De Profundis

Winston S. Churchill

c/o Rev. Welldon

Harrow-on-the-Hill

WITH HIS FELLOW HARROVIANS [FAR LEFT].

'A MERE SOCIAL WASTREL'

Lord Randolph determined that his eldest son would go into the army. Churchill remembered this decision being taken after a rare parental inspection of his large toy soldier collection. Winston hoped that his father had discerned in him the qualities of a 'military genius', an echo perhaps of his ancestor the famous 1st Duke of Marlborough, but it is more likely that Lord Randolph thought his son too stupid and erratic to go to university and considered him in need of discipline. Winston was enrolled in the Army class at Harrow but it still took him three attempts to pass the entrance examinations for Sandhurst, the military training college for officers. Even then, when he did finally succeed, it was not with enough marks to join a prestigious infantry regiment. This did not bother Winston, who was already a keen rider and eager to join the cavalry. But, when he wrote to his parents, any sense of achievement must have been wiped out by the damning letter he received back from his father.

Winston was on holiday with his brother Jack in Switzerland when the storm broke. His mother had tried to prepare him for it, writing 'Papa is not very pleased at y[ou]r getting in by the skin of y[ou]r teeth and missing the Infantry by 18 marks. He is not as pleased over y[ou]r exploits as you seem to be!' This was a huge understatement.

In his letter, Lord Randolph accuses Churchill of demonstrating a 'slovenly happy-go-lucky harum scarum style of work', threatens to cut him off and concludes that Winston 'will become a mere social wastrel, one of the hundreds of the public school failures, and … will degenerate into a shabby, unhappy and futile existence. If that is so you will have to bear all the blame for such misfortunes yourself.' It is difficult to imagine a more scathing letter from father to son. Yet while it does undoubtedly reflect the breakdown of their personal relationship, Lady Randolph's letter, written from the spa town of Bad Kissingen in Germany where Lord Randolph was undergoing treatment, also hints that Randolph had health problems. Winston did not yet know how serious they were or how profoundly they would impact his own life.

At the same time, his relationship with his mother was beginning to develop. In his subsequent letter from Sandhurst, he opens up to her about her criticisms of his letters, Lord Randolph's treatment of him as 'that boy' and refers to his own attempts at physical self-improvement, despite being 'cursed with so feeble a body, that I can hardly support the fatigues of the day'.

12: from Lady Randolph to Winston, 7 August 1893 (CHAR 1/8/45-46)

Hotel Victoria
Kissingen
Monday 7[th] August [1893]

Dearest Winston,

We have just received y[ou]r letters, & are very pleased to think you are enjoying yourselves– I am glad of course that you have got into Sandhurst but Papa is not very pleased at y[ou]r getting in by the skin of y[ou]r teeth & missing the Infantry by 18 marks. He is not as pleased over y[ou]r exploits as you seem to be!

...

Best love – & look after y[ou]rself & Jack.
Your loving Mother
JSC

13: from Lord Randolph to Winston, 9 August 1893 (CHAR 1/2/66-68)
9 Aug. 1893

My dear Winston,

I am rather surprised at your tone of exultation over your inclusion in the Sandhurst list. There are two ways of winning in an examination, one creditable the other the reverse. You have unfortunately chosen the latter method, and appear to be much pleased with your success.

The first extremely discreditable feature of your performance was missing the infantry, for in that failure is demonstrated beyond refutation your slovenly happy-go-lucky harum scarum style of work for which you have always been distinguished at your different schools. Never have I received a really good report of your conduct in your work from any master or tutor you had from time to time to do with. Always behind-hand, never advancing in your class, incessant complaints of total want of application.

. . .

With all the advantages you had, with all the abilities which you foolishly think yourself to possess & which some of your relations claim for you, with all the efforts that have been made to make your life easy & agreeable & your work neither oppressive or distasteful, this is the grand result that you come up among the 2nd rate & 3rd rate class who are only good for commissions in a cavalry regiment.

. . .

Do not think I am going to take the trouble of writing to you long letters after every folly & failure you commit & undergo. I shall not write again on these matters & you need not trouble to write any answer to this part of my letter, because I no longer attach the slightest weight to anything you may say about your own acquirements & exploits. Make this position indelibly impressed on your mind, that if your conduct & action at Sandhurst is similar to what it has been in the other establishments in which it has sought vainly to impart to you some education, then that my responsibility for you is over.

I shall leave you to depend on yourself giving you merely such assistance as may be necessary to permit of a respectable life. Because I am certain that if you cannot prevent yourself from leading the idle useless unprofitable life you have had during your schooldays & later months, you will become a mere social wastrel one of the hundreds of the public school failures, and you will degenerate into a shabby unhappy & futile existence.

. . .

Your affectionate father,
Randolph S.C.

Kissingen

August 9 1893

My dear Winston I am rather surprised
at your tone of exultation over your
inclusion in the Sandhurst list. There
are two ways of winning in an examination, one creditable
the other the reverse. You have unfortunately
chosen the latter method, and
appear to be much pleased with your
success.

The first entirely discreditable
feature of your performance was
of missing the infantry,
now that failure is demonstrated
beyond refutation your slovenly
happy-go-lucky harum scarum style

a mere social wastrel one of the
hundreds of the public school
failures, you will degenerate into a
shabby unhappy & futile existence.
If that is so you will have
to bear all the blame for such
misfortunes yourself. Your
own conscience will enable you to
recall & enumerate all the
efforts that have been made
I give you the best of chances

by your position
which you were entitled to a time
you have practically neglected them all
I hope you will be the better
for your trip. You must apply
apply to Capt & James & do so your
Sandhurst requirements. Your
mother sends her love
Your affte father
Randolph S C

LORD RANDOLPH CHURCHILL.

14: from Winston to Lady Randolph, 17 September 1893 (CHAR 28/19/13-15)

Sept. 17 [1893]

My dear Mamma,

Your letter arrived last night, and made me feel rather unhappy. I am awfully sorry that Papa does not approve of my letters. I take a great deal of pains over them & often re-write entire pages. If I write a descriptive account of my life here, I receive a hint from you that my style is too sententious & stilted. If on the other hand I write a plain & excessively simple letter – it is put down as slovenly. I never can do anything right.

. . .

As to the leave – it is very hard that Papa cannot grant me the same liberty that other boys in my position are granted. It is only a case of trusting me. As my Company Officer said he "likes to know the boys whom their parents could trust" & therefore recommended me to get permission sorted for. However it is no use my trying to explain to Papa, & I suppose I shall go on being treated as "that boy" till I am 50 years old.

...

It is a great pleasure to me to write to you unreservedly instead of having to pick & choose my words & information. So far I have been extremely good. Neither late nor lazy, & have had always 5 minutes to wait before each parade or study.

Yesterday I went out riding with a charming Eton boy (he is 19½) whose acquaintance I have made. We got to Aldershot & were having a stiff gallop when his saddle slipped round & he fell on his head. Of course he was stunned & for now got concussions of the brain. I revived him as well as I could – with brandy & water then had to hire a cab to drive all the way back to Sandhurst. I took him to see a doctor on the road who said he had had a marvellous escape of breaking his neck. The whole thing was a great responsibility & [rather an] experience.

...

Well I have told you all about my life. I am cursed with so feeble a body, that I can hardly support the fatigues of the day; but I suppose I shall get stronger during my stay here.

...

Good-bye dear darling Mamma. Ever so much love & more kisses,

From your ever loving son,
Winston S. Churchill.

'PAPA WROTE ME A LONG LETTER ABOUT THE WATCH AND SEEMS TO BE VERY CROSS'
Winston seems to have enjoyed his time at Sandhurst, especially the practical work and the riding, describing it as 'a new start'.

Unfortunately, attempts to reset the relationship with his father went badly wrong when he dropped the expensive watch Randolph had given him in a pond. It was recovered, with the help of a troop who drained the water, and was sent to be repaired. All might have been well had not the family watchmaker then mentioned to Lord Randolph that this was the second time he had been asked to mend Winston's watch. Lord Randolph was incensed and wrote this letter to his son, calling him a 'young stupid' and comparing him unfavourably to his younger brother Jack who 'in all qualities of steadiness taking care of his things & never doing stupid things' is 'vastly your superior'.

Churchill's letter of explanation to his mother shows his concern. It is clear from his later writings and from conversations with his own children that Churchill craved his father's approval above all else. In 1894 he still harboured hopes of helping Lord Randolph in his political work and of impressing his father with his own military career. Unfortunately, it was too late. Lord Randolph's career was already over. The tone and poor handwriting of his letter to his son contain strong clues that all was not well with his health.

15: from Lord Randolph to Winston, 21 April 1894 (CHAR 1/2/78)
21 Apr 1894

Dear Winston,

I have received you letter of yesterdays [sic] date & am glad to learn that you are getting on well in your work. But I heard something about you yesterday which annoyed & vexed me very much. I was at Mr Dent's about my watch, and he told me of the shameful way in which you had misused the very valuable watch which I gave you. He told me that you had sent it to him some time ago, having with the utmost carelessness dropped it on a stone pavement & broken it badly. The repairs of it cost £3.17s. which you will have to pay Mr Dent. He then told me he had again received the watch the other day and that you told him it had been dropped in the water. He told me that the whole of the watch was horribly rusty & that every bit of the watch had had to be taken to pieces. I would not believe you could be such a young stupid. It is clear you are not to be trusted with a valuable watch & when I get it from Mr Dent I shall not give it you back. You had better buy one of those cheap watches for £2 as those are the only ones which if you smash are not v[er]y costly to replace. Jack has had the watch I gave him longer than you have had yours; the only expense I have paid on his watch was 10/s for cleaning before he went back to Harrow. But in all qualities of steadiness taking care of his things & never doing stupid things Jack is vastly your superior.

Your v[er]y much worried parent,
Randolph S. Churchill

16: from Winston to Lady Randolph, 24 April 1894 (CHAR 28/20/16)

ROYAL MILITARY COLLEGE,
SANDHURST.
Apr. 24.

My dearest Mamma,

Thank you so much for your letter – which I have just received. Papa wrote me a long letter about the watch and seems to be very cross. I wrote back at once saying how sorry I was and explaining the whole affair & got a letter by return of post – last night. I think that by his letter Papa is somewhat mollified. I hope so indeed. But how on earth could I help it. I have no waistcoat to put the watch in and so have had to wear it in the pocket of my tunic.

Papa writes, he is sending me a Waterbury [a make of watch] – which is rather a come down. I am very sorry it should have happened – as you can well believe – and sorrier still that Papa should have heard of it. But I feel quite clear in my own mind that I am not to blame except for having brought so good a watch back here – where there is everything in the way of its safety.

...

I remain,
Ever your loving son,
Winston S. Churchill

JENNIE SPENCER-CHURCHILL, 1888.

'I HAD NEVER REALISED HOW ILL PAPA HAD BEEN'

Churchill's father was in fact in the grip of a terminal illness. He was being treated for syphilis, though some medical historians have suggested it may have been a brain tumour. Churchill only found out very late. His parents were away on a final world tour, designed to keep Lord Randolph away from London society, when he persuaded Dr Roose to tell him all. Churchill's hopes that his father's relapse might prove temporary were dashed and Lord Randolph returned to Britain to die. The end came on 24 January 1895. He was only forty-five.

Lord Randolph's death was one of the defining moments of Churchill's life. It acted as a catalyst, spurring him into a political career of his own in which he could prove himself to his father's memory. It gave him the sense of mission that he had hitherto lacked while focusing his mind on how short his own life might be. In the coming years, he would write his father's biography and seek to emulate his achievements. Shortly after the Second World War, when he

had little to prove to anyone, he wrote a short essay called 'The
Dream' in which he imagined (perhaps dreamed) a conversation
with Lord Randolph's ghost. Even then, the spectre disappeared
in a puff of cigarette smoke before Winston could explain his own
role in the momentous events of the mid-twentieth century. Jock
Colville, Winston's long-serving private secretary, thought it was no
coincidence that Churchill's final illness only ended on 24 January
1965, seventy years to the day after the death of his father.

However, we must not get ahead of ourselves. In 1895, his father's
death signalled the end of Churchill's childhood. Winston was just
twenty years old. The stubborn, fiercely independent, slightly needy,
slightly sickly red-headed child with a penchant for the dramatic, a
thirst for adventure and a good vocabulary now needed to make his
own way in the world.

17: from Winston to Lady Randolph, 2 November 1894
(CHAR 28 / 20 / 45-46)

2 Nov. 1894
50 Grosvenor Square.
W.
Nov. 2

My dearest Mamma,

I hope that everything is still going on well. A telegram from
Singapore yesterday – announced papa's arrival – and said that
everything was all right. I persuaded Dr Roose to tell me exactly
how Papa was – as I thought it was only right that I should know
exactly how he was progressing.

. . .

. . . he told me everything and showed me the medical reports . . .
and I beg you above all things not to write to Roose on the subject
of his having told me as he told it [to] me in confidence.

. . .

I need not tell you how anxious I am. I had never realised how
ill Papa had been and had never until now believed that there was

anything serious the matter. I do trust & hope as sincerely as human beings can that the relapse Keith spoke of in his last report was only temporary and that the improvement of the past few months has been maintained.

. . .

Now about yourself. Darling mummy I do hope that you are keeping well and that the fatigues of travelling as well as the anxiety you must feel about Papa – are not telling on you. I can't tell you how I long to see you again and how I look forward to your return. Do what you can with Papa to induce him to allow me to come out and join you.

. . .

Well good bye my darling dearest Mummy.
With best of love & kisses,
I remain,
Ever your loving and affectionate son,
<u>Winston</u>

PORTRAIT OF LORD RANDOLPH CHURCHILL.

CHAPTER TWO

THOUGHTS AND ADVENTURES
(1895–99)

'IT IS A FINE GAME TO PLAY – THE GAME OF POLITICS'
And so the next phase of Churchill's life began. Based in barracks
at Aldershot in Hampshire, Churchill plunged into regimental life.
In this letter to his mother, now his most regular correspondent,
he describes being in the 'midst of manoeuvres' and spending all
of his time in the saddle at exercises or playing polo. But he then
switches tack and writes about his cousin Sunny, who has just
become the 9th Duke of Marlborough and delivered his maiden
(first) speech in the House of Lords. Perhaps we can detect a hint
of envy, particularly when Winston ponders how his father would
have liked to have seen the moment.

'The more I see of soldiering – the more I like it', Winston
writes, and yet in the same breath he recognizes that it is not his
'métier' (his vocation). He is only twenty years of age, and he has
only been a soldier for a few months, but he already knows that it is
not where his heart or perhaps his true talents lie. 'It is a fine game
to play – the game of politics – and it is well worth waiting for a
good hand – before really plunging in.'

Churchill was already determined to swap his sword for a political
despatch box and become a Member of Parliament. In this letter he
talks about gaining 'four years of healthy & pleasant existence' in
the army with discipline and responsibility, but that was never going
to be the Churchill way. Much of the next five years would be spent
travelling the globe in pursuit of fame and fortune.

1: from Winston to Lady Randolph, 16 August 1895
(CHAR 28 / 21 / 59-61)

Aug. 16 [1895]

My dearest Mummy,

   ...

We are now in the midst of manoeuvres. Eight hours in the saddle every day – then two hours stables and then to Polo indefatigably. This new Inspector General of Cavalry is a terror & every one goes about in dread of him – excepting only the Colonel who is in high favour & commands (temporarily) a Brigade.

   ...

I suppose you will have read the speech in which Sunny Marlborough moved the vote of thanks in return for the address. It appears to have been a very good and even brilliant speech & I was told he had a very good delivery – though a trifle too loud for the House. I don't care to dwell on the past – but I could not help thinking as I read it – that Papa would have liked to see that he inherited at least some of the family talents – and was trying quietly and tactfully to use them.

   ...

It is a fine game to play – the game of politics – and it is well worth waiting for a good hand – before really plunging in.

At any rate – four years of healthy & pleasant existence – combined with both responsibility & discipline – can do no harm to me – but rather good. The more I see of soldiering – the more I like it – but the more I feel convinced that it is not my métier. Well, we shall see – my dearest Mamma –

   ...

Well au revoir – my dear Mamma.
With best love and kisses
I remain
Your loving son
Winston S. Churchill

POSING WITH HIS MOTHER, IN HIS EARLY TWENTIES.

'WHAT AN EXTRAORDINARY PEOPLE THE AMERICANS ARE'

In the winter of 1895, Churchill and his friend and fellow officer Reginald Barnes used their army leave to seek adventure. Exploiting Lord and Lady Randolph's network of contacts, they got themselves attached to the Spanish force seeking to put down the Cuban national uprising. Lady Randolph, born in Brooklyn, leapt into action. She arranged for Winston to stay with her friend (and possibly former lover) Bourke Cockran. The famous American politician and orator lived on Fifth Avenue and took on the role of mentor, introducing Winston to Manhattan high society.

Churchill spent an impressionable week in New York, being wined and dined. He was not impressed with West Point (the American Sandhurst), where he thought the officer cadets were too controlled, disliked the American paper dollar, and, as an aspiring writer and journalist, was particularly scathing about the quality of the newspapers. To his mother he wrote, 'What an extraordinary people the Americans are! Their hospitality is a revelation to me and they make you feel at home and at ease in a way that I have never before experienced. On the other hand their press and their currency impress me very unfavourably.'

In a letter to his brother Jack, he elaborated: 'But the essence of American Journalism is vulgarity divested of truth. Their best papers write for a class of snotty housemaids and footmen ... I think – mind you that vulgarity is sign of strength. A great, crude, strong, young people are the Americans – like a boisterous healthy boy among enervated but well bred ladies and gentlemen.' Of course, his cousin Sunny was being attacked in the American press at the time for his marriage to Consuelo Vanderbilt.

This would be the first of many visits to his mother's homeland. The ensuing trip to Cuba saw Churchill celebrate his twenty-first birthday while on operations. He came under fire and wrote up his experiences as his first newspaper articles. Churchill's military and literary career had begun, but his adventures were about to be temporarily curtailed. His regiment, the 4th Hussars, was posted to garrison duty in India.

2: from Winston to his brother, Jack Churchill, 15 November 1895 (CHAR 28/21/85-89)

763 5th Avenue
New York
Nov. 15 [1895]

My dearest Jack,

   ...

I am still staying with Mr Bourke Cockran, whom you met in Paris, in his very comfortable and convenient flat in 5th Avenue ... On Sunday we start for Havana by the route of Philadelphia – Washington – Savannah – Tampa Bay & Key West – arriving there on Wednesday morning all being well.

Mr Cockran, who has great influence over here, procured us orders to visit the Forts of the Harbour and West Point – which is the American Sandhurst.

I am sure you will be horrified by some Regulations of the Military Academy. The cadets enter from 19-22 & stay 4 years. This means that they are most of them 24 years of age. They are not allowed to smoke or have any money in their possession nor are they given any leave except 2 months after the 1st two years. In fact they have far less liberty than any <u>private</u> school boys in our country. I think such a state of things is positively disgraceful and young men of 24 or 25 who would resign their personal liberty to such an extent can never make good citizens or fine soldiers. A child who rebels against that sort of control should be whipped – so should a man who does not rebel.

. . .

This is a very great country – my dear Jack. Not pretty or romantic – but great and utilitarian. There seems to be no such thing as reverence or tradition. Everything is eminently practical and things are judged from a matter of fact standpoint. Take for instance the Courthouse. No robes or wigs or uniformed workers – Nothing but a lot of men in black coats & tweed suits – Judge prisoner jury counsel & wardens all indiscriminately mixed.

. . .

I saw Sunny last night & am dining with the Vanderbilts this evening. He is very pleased with himself and seems very fit. The newspapers have abused him scurrilously. But the essence of American Journalism is vulgarity divested of truth. Their best papers write for a class of snotty housemaids and footmen & even the nicest people here have so much vitiated their taste as to appreciate the style.

I think – mind you that vulgarity is sign of strength. A great, crude, strong, young people are the Americans – like a boisterous healthy boy among enervated but well bred ladies and gentlemen. Some day Jack when you are older – you must come out here and I think you will feel as I feel – and think as I think today.

. . .

With best love –
Ever your loving brother
Winston S. Churchill

CHURCHILL, THE WAR CORRESPONDENT, C. 1899.

'BURN THIS JACK WITHOUT SHOWING TO ANYONE'

Churchill arrived in India in October 1896 and took up residence in Bangalore. It was here, between routine army duties and playing polo, that he felt 'the desire for learning' come upon him. Realizing that his education to date had been inadequate, he started to read widely in history, philosophy and economics. No doubt this pleased his Harrow headmaster, the Reverend Welldon, and the two exchanged letters. This did not mean of course that Churchill was prepared to agree with everything his former teacher wrote. Never a great believer in organized religion, and always stubbornly independent in his thought, he disagreed with Welldon's support for missionary work, arguing that 'Providence has given each man the form of worship best suited to his food and climate' and that religious change had normally been accompanied by blood and controversy.

The letter shows Churchill starting to think for himself and to formulate his views. His reference to the '<u>innate upward</u> striving ...

inherent in an elementary proto-plasmic cell' hints at his familiarity with new scientific ideas, like Charles Darwin's theory of evolution. Churchill later wrote that he was passing 'through a violent and aggressive anti-religious phase which, had it lasted, might easily have made me a nuisance'. His views on religion and science at this time became intertwined with his views on race (which are unacceptable to a modern audience). He believed that the Europeans were best adapted to Christianity because it was a higher form of religion. Churchill's belief in the British Empire and racial hierarchies was also strengthened by his experiences as a white officer in India.

It is not clear whether Churchill sent this letter. Maybe he lacked the confidence to argue at this level with Welldon. Though he did send a copy to his brother Jack, who was still at Harrow, perhaps as a way of showing off that he was now on equal terms with the headmaster. As for Welldon, he would later practise what he had preached about missionary work, becoming Bishop of Calcutta.

3: from Winston to the Reverend James Welldon, Headteacher at Harrow, 16 December 1896 (draft) (CHAR 28 / 152A / 85-86)

Bangalore.
Dec. 16th. [18]96
Copy.
Burn this Jack without showing to anyone.

My dear Mr Welldon,

...

My chief reason for deprecating missionary work I find in the belief that – 'Providence has given each man the form of worship best suited to his food and climate'. I imagine that this religion was originally evolved in process of time – by the influence of material forces – climate & physical – acting on the <u>innate upward</u> striving by which all human beings are impelled – and which, I am told, is inherent in an elementary proto-plasmic cell.

. . .

... You have written that "It is not stranger that a religion issuing from London should naturalize itself in Calcutta than that a religion, issuing from Jerusalem should have naturalized itself in London." Will you forgive me if I say that it seems to me that the analogy is not quite just? The barriers that have divided the religions – I have alluded to – have never been broken. Christianity originated in a city of the Roman Empire – among <u>white</u> men – and spread thence <u>northwards</u>. As it found a grateful soil everywhere – it follows – to my mind – that it is the religion best adapted to the spiritual need of the European inhabitants of the North Temperate Zone. But in nearly nineteen centuries it has not spread south or east ... Centuries of missionary enterprise in China have been barren: and in this country the proselytes are chiefly servants aspiring to situations With Europeans. Nor have the religions of Buddha – Mahomet – & Confucius gained a single white convert.

Let me ~~finally at~~ in conclusion state my thesis more moderately and if possible more firmly. Religion is natural to man – but some races are capable of a higher and purer form than others. I believe that the Asiatic derives more real benefit from the perfect knowledge & practice of his own religion – albeit inferior – than from the imperfect and partial comprehension of Christianity.

I hope you will forgive me for the freedom and length of this letter. I have in vain aspired to the terseness and conciseness of your argument. The day has passed agreeably in thinking out this letter – and I shall consider it well spent if you are induced to write to me again.

. . .

Yours most affectionately
Winston S. Churchill.

. . .

CHURCHILL ATOP A HORSE-DRAWN CARRIAGE IN BANGALORE, 1894.

'TO BEAT MY SWORD INTO A PAPER CUTTER'

Christmas 1896 found Churchill in an ill mood. He had gone to Calcutta to attend the horse races but found himself suffering from a bad leg, a cold and a clear dose of homesickness. The bad leg at least gave him an excuse from any dancing, but he vented his frustration about the British expatriate civilian community, describing them as 'supremely uninteresting people'. This may be in part the natural prejudice of the headstrong, young military officer who wanted to see action (he was trying to get his mother to help him transfer to Egypt at the time). However, there was always an element of Churchill that was not sociable; he did not make close friends easily and if he could not be at the centre of events then he preferred his own company. He refers to his love of 'roses – polo ponies – & butterflies'. This admiration for nature would stay with him and in later life he would derive huge pleasure from the gardens and wildlife at Chartwell, his home in Kent.

Once again, there may be an element of jealousy in Churchill's description of his cousin Sunny, the Duke of Marlborough, and his successful social climbing back at Blenheim. Winston wanted to exchange his army sword for a politician's paper cutter, and his sabretache (military satchel) for an election address.

Any early love affair with India was over and his frustrations, unhappiness and refusal to engage with the country left a lingering resentment and hostility that would resurface.

ON HORSEBACK, BANGALORE, 1897.

4: from Winston to Lady Randolph, 23 December 1896 (CHAR 28/22/37)
Continental Hotel, Calcutta

Dec. 23. 96

My dearest Mamma.

After a prosperous voyage we are arrived here – and Hugo & I have tolerably comfortably rooms in this pretentious hotel. A Mr Hewett of the Bengal Civil Service – who I met at Deepdene – has amiably had us made honorary members of the Club – a very good one – and generally looks after us. My knee is still so bad as to make me as lame as a cat and indeed I fear that it will take at least a fortnight for the wound to heal completely. Calcutta is very full of supremely uninteresting people endeavouring to assume an air of 'heartiness' suitable to the season ... the instant I get into an Indian Club – or into any situation where I am confronted with [the] spectacle of the Anglo-Indian at home – I immediately desire to fly the country. It is only in my comfortable bungalow – among my roses – polo ponies – & butterflies – that I feel that philosophical composure – which can alone make residence in India endurable ...

...

I see the papers full of pictures of the Blenheim festivities: Sunny gloating over the Prince's marksmanship the most prominent. The whole business appears to have been very satisfactory – and is bound to do Marlborough a great deal of good. There is always a great name to be made by the judicious application of wealth – and he is just the person to do it.

...

I revolve Egypt continuously in my mind. There are many pros and cons – but I feel bound to take it if I can get it. To-day with cold and quinine I feel that England would be the happiest solution of the question – as to where I should soldier. However I daresay dinner will have an elevating effect and induce me to take more rosy views. Two years in Egypt my dearest Mamma – with a campaign thrown in – would I think qualify me to be allowed to beat my sword into a paper cutter & my sabretache into an election address. Such a stupid letter – but how can I help it! Ammoniated quinine!

Ever your loving son,
Winston

'YOU CANNOT BUT FEEL ASHAMED OF YOURSELF'
Churchill may have felt isolated in India but that does not mean he would have enjoyed receiving every letter from home. In February 1897, his mother discovered that he had spent all of his allowance and run up very considerable additional debts. Her disappointment is clear. She tells him that he must manage his own affairs, that he seems to have no real purpose in life and that he should 'realize at the age

of 22 that for a man life means work, & hard work'. She opposes his desire to visit England, reminding him that he has only been in India for six months and that people will say that he 'can't stick to anything'.

It was often said of Churchill that he was 'easily satisfied with the best'. He liked living in luxury, even if he could not always pay for it, and saw money as a means to an end (unlike his brother Jack who was more level-headed and became a stockbroker). Trapped in India, with no action to relieve the boredom, he was living with two friends, Reginald Barnes and Hugo Baring, in a huge bungalow with two acres of land, many servants, a barn, and stables for thirty horses. Any money left over after paying for all of this was spent on his passion – polo. The 4th Hussars were determined to be the first regiment from southern India to win the prestigious Inter-Regimental Cup (a dream that would come true in 1899 just before Churchill left the army) and Churchill was one of their best players.

Lady Randolph lamented that 'Many men at your age have to work for a living & support their mother.' However, as we will see, she was far from prudent herself and much more like her eldest son than her letter suggests. At this stage, he was dependent on his allowance from home and his army salary, but he would soon devise a new way of earning money – by writing.

FAMILY PORTRAIT, LADY RANDOLPH, WINSTON AND JACK.

5: from Lady Randolph to Winston, 26 February 1897 (CHAR 1/8/91-93)

26 February 1897   35a Gt Cumberland Place

Dearest Winston ... I went to Cox's this morning & find out that not only you have anticipated the whole of y[ou]r quarter's allowance due this month but £45 besides – & now this cheque for £50 – & that <u>you knew</u> you had nothing at the bank. The manager told me they had warned you that they would not let you overdraw & the next mail brought this cheque. I <u>must</u> say I think it is <u>too</u> bad of you – indeed it is hardly honourable knowing as you do that you are dependent on me & that I give you the biggest allowance I possibly can, more than I can afford.

...

If you cannot live on y[ou]r allowance from me & y[ou]r pay you will have to leave the 4th Hussars. I <u>cannot</u> increase y[ou]r allowance.

As for y[ou]r wild talk & scheme of coming home for a month, it is absolutely out of the question, not only on account of money, but for the sake of y[ou]r reputation. They will say & with some reason that you can't stick to anything. You have only been out 6 months & it is on the cards that you may be called to Egypt. There is plenty for you to do in India.

I confess I am quite disheartened about you. You seem to have no real purpose in life & won't realize at the age of 22 that for a man life means work, & hard work if you mean to succeed. Many men at y[ou]r age have to work for a living & support their mother ... I will only repeat that I cannot help you any more & if you have any grit in you & are worth y[ou]r salt you will try & live within y[ou]r income & cut down y[ou]r expenses in order to do it ...

Y[ou]r Mother

JSC

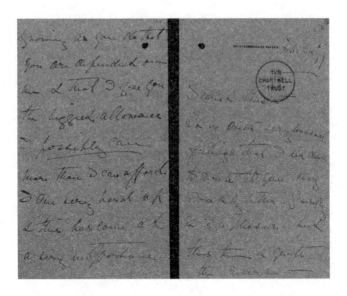

'I AM A LIBERAL IN ALL BUT NAME'

Health, money and politics. Churchill was now concerned about all of them. In April 1897 he was wounded on the rifle range, a bullet splintering on the iron edge of the target, damaging his hand and narrowly missing his eye. His admission to his mother of an aversion to physical pain suggests that he compensated by exercising considerable will power. Though not when it came to money. In spite of his mother's earlier letter, he had now run up considerable bills in two continents. Living as a cavalry officer was certainly not cheap and almost impossible to do on an army salary, as gentlemen were expected to have private wealth. However, Churchill consistently lived beyond his means. He was borrowing money from Indian moneylenders and still planning an expensive trip to England.

Churchill was angered by the refusal of the British government to do more to support the Greek uprising in Crete against the Ottoman Turks. He was firmly for the Greeks and even in favour of allowing the Russians to take Constantinople [Istanbul] and drive the Turks out of Europe. It led him to assert that he was a Liberal in all but name and to set out his political views. This statement of beliefs was a direct result of his self-education in India, where he had been reading reports of parliamentary debates and researching his father's political career. Lord Randolph Churchill had coined the term 'Tory Democracy' for a new form of popular Conservatism but had not lived to define it. For Winston it meant reform at home, imperialism abroad, non-intervention in Europe, all protected by the power of the mighty British Navy and guaranteed by the existing constitution.

The juxtaposition of reform at home and Empire abroad would become a constant refrain in Churchill's career. In 1897, it situated him somewhere between the main Conservative and Liberal parties, a strange mixture of reformer and reactionary and full of contradictions. He is prepared to support giving the vote to all men (but no mention of women), to strengthen local government, tax the rich and improve working conditions for the poor, but was opposed to greater freedoms for India. On Europe, his views would change, and he would go on to play a leading role in the two world wars that saw Britain intervene on the continent (and he would definitely change his mind about encouraging Russian expansion).

6: from Winston to Lady Randolph, 6 April 1897 (CHAR 28 / 23 / 31-33A)

Bangalore.
April 6th

My dearest Mamma,

We live in a world of strange experiences. In Cuba it was my fortune to be under fire, without being wounded. At Bangalore I have been wounded without being under fire. Four days ago I was in charge of the markers in the rifle butts and was sitting on the seat provided, thinking myself perfectly safe – when a bullet struck the iron edge of the Target – flew into splinters & rebounded all over me. One entered my left hand near the thumb and penetrated an inch and a half. Several others stuck in my khaki coat and many whistled all around. It is to the mercy of God – as some would say – or to the workings of chance or the doctrine of averages – as others prefer, that I was not hit in the eye; in this case I should have been blinded infallibly. Followed an abominable twenty minutes – probing etc – before the splinter was extracted & since then I have had a bad time every morning when the wound has to be syringed. Knowing, as you do, my keen aversion to physical pain – or even discomfort – I am sure you will sympathise with me.

I am now indeed a cripple ... However I am healing beautifully ... The mail this morning brought me your letter of the 18th March. I am indeed sorry that my cheque was dishonoured ...

I don't know what will happen in the near future. I must raise a certain sum of money on a life insurance or some other security & pay off these pressing liabilities lest I obtain a most unenviable reputation ...

...

I [am] sorry you do not agree with my views on Crete. Certainly I have seen no reason to alter what I wrote. We are doing a very wicked thing in firing on the Cretan insurgents & in blockading Greece – so that she cannot succour them. It will take a lot of whitewash to justify the spectacle of the Seaforth Highlanders fighting by the side of the Bashi Bazouk [Ottoman troops] ...

We have more ships & more men on the spot and generally appear to be taking a very leading part. So what? In a most atrocious crime. Where France & Germany have hesitated, we have rushed in. I am quite sure the people of England do not approve of the use to which their fleets and armies are being put – and the Government will most certainly have to answer for their conduct.

...

This is not only wrong but foolish, it is wrong because it is unjustifiable to kill people who are not attacking you – because their continued existence is inconvenient: and because it is an abominable action, which prolongs the servitude under the Turks of the Christian races.

...

After all – we do not live in Crimean War days – nor need we repeat the follies of the past. Russia must have Constantinople. It is the birthplace of her religion & the aim of her ambitions ... We shall be [foolish] mad if we attempt to bar the just aspirations of a mighty people ...

...

Our Machiavellian Government had better be careful lest they find themselves even outdone in vice. There are not lengths to which I would not go in opposing them – were I in the House of Commons. I am a Liberal in all but name. My views excite the pious horror of the mess. Were it not for Home Rule [for Ireland] – to which I will never consent – I would enter Parliament as a Liberal. As it is – Tory Democracy will have to be the standard under which I shall range myself.

1 <u>Reform at home</u>. Extension of the Franchise to every male. Universal Education. Equal Establishment of all religions. Wide measures of local self government. Eight hours. Payment of Members (on request). A progressive Income Tax ... I will vote for them all.

2 Imperialism abroad.
East of Suez Democratic reins are impossible. India must be governed on old principles. The colonies must be federated & a system of Imperial Defence arranged. Also we must combine for Tariff & Commerce.

3 European Politics
Non Intervention. Keep absolutely unembroiled – Isolated if you like.

4 Defence
The colonies must contribute and hence a council must be formed. A mighty navy must keep the seas. The army

may be reduced to a training depot for India with one
army corps for petty expeditions.

5 To maintain the present constitution of Queen – Lords –
Commons – & the Legislative Union as at present established.

There! That is creed of Tory Democracy. Peace & Power abroad –
Prosperity & Progress at home – will be the results.

Ever your loving son
Winston

'I HAVE FAITH IN MY STAR'

From the moment of his arrival in India, Churchill was pushing to
get away from the boring routine of garrison duty in Bangalore.
He wanted to see action and try and make a name for himself.
His opportunity came in August 1897 when General Sir Bindon
Blood invited him to join the Malakand Field Force, an expedition
on the North-West Frontier to subdue a rising by the local tribes
in what is now Pakistan and Afghanistan. Churchill leapt at the
chance, persuading the British *Daily Telegraph* and Indian *Allahabad
Pioneer* newspapers to pay him for his reports from the front. These
commissions were important to him, not just as a source of funding
but also as a way of getting noticed and making a name for himself.

Writing to his mother before the fighting, on 5 September, he
expressed his 'faith in my star' and his belief that he was 'intended
to do something in the world', being prepared to play the odds and
risk death or a life-changing wound in return for a chance of fame.
Two weeks later he was able to report on what had happened. He
had been involved in a fierce action, in which he had seen those on
both sides killed (and had possibly killed others himself), but had
'felt no excitement and very little fear'. He describes riding 'on my
grey pony all along the skirmish line where everyone else was lying
down in cover. Foolish perhaps – but I play for high stakes and given
an audience – there is no act too daring or too noble. Without the
gallery – things are different.'

Churchill's letters capture the horrors and brutality of war, but also reveal that he thrived under this pressure and was determined to use the experience. As a result, he was cross when the *Telegraph* printed his letters as being from 'a young officer', without giving his name. It led him to write up his adventures as his first book, *The Story of the Malakand Field Force*. He also used his experiences to inform his only novel, *Savrola*, even though he later advised his friends not to read it.

7: from Winston to Lady Randolph, 5 September 1897 (CHAR 28/23/52)

Malakand Camp – 5th Sept. [1897]

My dearest Mamma,

. . .

So much for business – my dearest Mamma, my letters to the D[aily]T[elegraph] will explain most things that are going on here. I live with Sir Bindon Blood – who is very kind to me. I am at present correspondent of the Pioneer to which I have to telegraph 300 words a day. At the first opportunity I am to be put on the strength of this force – which will give me a medal if I come through.

As to fighting – we march tomorrow, and before a week is out, there will be a battle – probably the biggest yet fought on the frontier this year. By the time this reaches you everything will be over so that I do not mind writing about it. I have faith in my star – that is that I am intended to do something in the world. If I am mistaken – what does it matter? My life has been a pleasant one and though I should regret to leave it – It would be a regret that perhaps I should never know.

At any rate you will understand that I am bound for many reasons to risk something,

Lord Fincastle here – will get a Victoria Cross for his courage in a recent action – and though of course I do not aspire to that, I am inclined to think that my chance of getting attached would be improved by my behaviour. In any case – I mean to play this game out and if I lose it is obvious that I never could have won any other. The unpleasant contingency is of course a wound which would leave permanent effects and would while leaving me life – deprive me of all that makes life worth living. But all games have forfeits. Fortunately the odds are good.

The movement wh[ich] takes place tomorrow is a little romantic. For more than a week we shall disappear from the world. We let go our hold on Telegraphs and communications & plunge into an unknown country – with an uncounted & unproved enemy. After a pause we shall emerge from the mountains near Peshawar – and thence form part of the force wh[ich] will be used against the Afridis and Orakzais. This may last about till Christmas – and after that there will possibly be 3 months leave to all engaged.

Good bye my dearest Mamma – I will arrange to have your letters forwarded. Do not worry. A philosophical temperament should transcend all human weaknesses – fear or affection.

Ever your loving son,
Winston S. Churchill
PS: I enclose Sir Bindon's letter

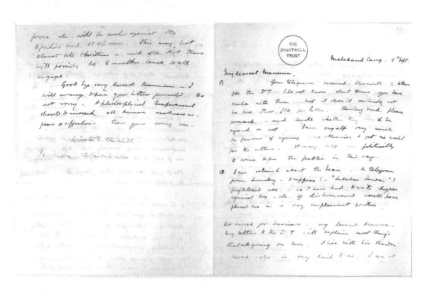

8: from the same, 19 September 1897 (CHAR 28 / 23 / 57)
Camp Inayat Kila 19 Sept

Dearest Mamma,

The enclosed 3 letters to the Daily Telegraph will tell you a good deal of what happened here ... But I must give you some account of my personal experiences of the 16th. I started with the Cavalry and saw the first shot fired. After half an hour's skirmishing I rode forward with the 35th Sikhs until firing got so hot that my grey pony was unsafe. I proceeded on foot. When the retirement began – I remained till the last and here I was perhaps very near my end. If you read between the lines of my letter you will see that this retirement was an awful rout in which the wounded were left to be cut horribly by these wild beasts. I was close to both officers when they were hit almost simultaneously and fired my revolver at a man at 30 yards who tried to cut up Poor Hughes' body. He dropped but came on again. A subaltern – Bethune by name and I carried a wounded sepoy for some distance and might perhaps, had there been any gallery, have received some notice. My pants are still stained with the mans [sic] blood. We also remained till the enemy came to within 40 yards firing our revolvers. They actually threw stones at us. It was a horrible business. For there was no help for the man that went down. I felt no excitement and very little fear. All the excitement went out when things became really deadly ...

Altogether I was shot at from 7.30 til 8. on this day – and now begin to consider myself a veteran.

Sir Bindon has made me his orderly officer, so that I shall get a medal & perhaps a couple of clasps.

...

I hope you can make out this scrawl dearest mamma – tell Jack details. In my novel I develop the idea that a 'politician' very often possesses mere physical courage. Military opinion is of course contrary. But at any rate – whatever I do afterwards – no one can say anything against me on this score. I rode on my grey pony all along the skirmish line where everyone else was lying down in cover. Foolish perhaps – but I play for high stakes and given an audience – there is no act too daring or too noble. Without the gallery – things are different.

I will write again soon – if all goes well – if not – you know my life has been a pleasant one. Quality not quantity is after all what we should strive for. Still I should like to come back and wear my medals at some big dinner or some other function.

... Europe is infinitely remote – England infinitely small – Bangalore – a speck on the map of India – but here everything is life size and flesh colour.

Ever your loving son
Winston

'IT IS NOT SO MUCH A QUESTION OF BRAINS AS OF CHARACTER & ORIGINALITY'

In the two letters that follow to his mother, we see Churchill's thoughts turning increasingly towards a future political career. They show that he has already learned two important lessons. First, that what counts is 'character and originality'. You need to have the public's confidence, but to gain it you need self-belief and to stand out from the crowd. And second, that you have to be heard.

Churchill may have described himself as 'a Liberal in all but name' but he was the son of a famous Conservative and his connections were all with the Tory Party. In January, Churchill was in touch with Conservative Central Office about becoming a candidate for Parliament and had already written his first election address, in case his father's old London constituency of Paddington became vacant.

In July, he used army leave to speak to the Conservatives at Bradford and was thrilled by his reception, describing it as 'a complete success' that had stirred his blood. He was particularly relieved that his speech impediment had proved no hindrance.

Churchill had a lifelong lisp and struggled to pronounce the letter 'S'. In later life, he would turn this to his advantage, using it to make his voice distinctive and instantly recognizable, for example by pronouncing Nazi as 'Narzee'. It is easy to forget that every public speaker has to start somewhere and the twenty-three-year-old was clearly nervous about whether he could address an audience and how he would be received. He studied public speaking, writing an essay called 'Scaffolding of Rhetoric', and Bradford was not his first political speech. He had spoken in Bath a year earlier, and while at Sandhurst he had delivered an off-the-cuff speech against the Purity Campaign of Mrs Ormiston Chant, who had attempted to segregate men and women in the Promenade of London's Empire Theatre. Winston and his fellow cadets had torn down the canvas screens designed to keep the two sexes apart and Churchill had spoken from the barricades. Yet Bradford was different. It was a self-imposed test to see if he could make a serious political speech. His success meant that his decision to resign his commission and leave the army was now definite: a matter of when, not if.

9: from Winston to Lady Randolph, 26 January 1898 (CHAR 28/24/26-29)

Jan 26th 1898

My dearest Mamma,

...

I am full of excitement to see the book and to read the proofs ...

The publication of the book will be certainly the most noteworthy act of my life. Up to date (of course). By its reception – I shall measure the chance of my possible success in the world. Although on a larger subject and with more time I am capable of a purer and more easy style and of more deeply considered views – yet it is a sample of my mental cast. If it goes down – then all may be well.

In Politics a man, I take it, gets on not so much by what he does, as by what he is. It is not so much a questions of brains as of character & originality. It is for these reasons that I would not allow others to suggest ideas and that I am somewhat impatient of advice as to my beginning in politics. Introduction – connections – powerful friends – a name – good advice well followed all these things count – but they lead only to a certain point. As it were they may ensure admission to the scales. Ultimately – every man has to be weighed – and if found wanting nothing can procure him the public confidence.

Nor would I desire it under such circumstances. If I am not good enough – others are welcome to take my place. I should never care to bolster up a sham reputation and hold my position by disguising my personality. Of course – as you have known for some time – I believe in myself. If I did not I might perhaps take other views.

I hope the book will please you. After all it is your applause that I covet more than any other. Indeed I think that would include all others. "A prophet is not without honour etc."

I shall send by next mail an Election address wh[ich] I have written. Captain Middleton advised me to leave one in his hands – in case of Paddington falling vacant – or a General Election unexpectedly occurring. Having read it – please send it to the offices. Unless, that is, you violently disapprove. I am afraid it is very 'blood and thunder' – but that is the usual style for such literature.

...

I want:-

1   Proofs of book – but don't wait for corrections – Print at once.
2   25 copies.
3   Long letters from you.
4   To go to Egypt.

Goodbye my dearest mamma,

Ever your loving son,

Winston S. Churchill

P.S. We are all thinking of the Big Polo Tournament now. But it fills a v[er]y different position in my mind to what it did last year.

Seventy thousand people have died of reported plague – Probably real figures double!!!

10: from the same, 15 July 1898 (CHAR 28 / 25 / 25-26)
Bradford

15 July [1898]

My dearest mamma,

The meeting was a complete success. The hall was not a v[er]y large one – but it was closely packed. I was listened to with the greatest attention for 55 minutes at the end of which time there were loud & general cries of "Go on". Five or six times they applauded for about two minutes without stopping and at the end of the peroration – which the newspapers cut owing to necessities of printing – many people mounted their chairs and there was really a very great deal of enthusiasm. In reply to a note of thanks – I said that I had already spoken for nearly an hour, and that only three minutes remained – whereupon they shouted "Go on for another hour" & "coom back lad" etc. All of which was v[er]y gratifying.

. . .

Personally – I was intensely pleased with the event. The keenness of the audience stirred my blood – and altho I stuck to my notes rigidly – I certainly succeeded in rousing & in amusing them. They burst out of the hall & pressed all round the carriage to shake hands and cheered till we had driven quite away.

The conclusions I form are these – with practice I shall obtain great power on a public platform. My impediment is no hindrance. My voice sufficiently powerful – and – this is vital – my ideas & modes of thought are pleasing to men.

It may be perhaps the hand of Fate – which by a strange coincidence closed one line of advance and aspiration in the morning – and in the evening pointed out another with an encouraging gesture. At any rate – my decision to resign my commission is definite.

With best love,

Your ever loving son,

Winston

P.S. They cheered you several times last night with great cordiality.

. . .

CHURCHILL SPEAKING IN DURBAN AFTER HIS ESCAPE FROM
BOER CAPTIVITY, 1899.

'WE BOTH KNOW WHAT IS GOOD – AND WE BOTH LIKE TO HAVE IT'

Yet it would still take time for Churchill to realize his dream of entering Parliament. One of the remaining problems was money. This time it was not Churchill who was spending it. Despite her earlier complaints about her son, Lady Randolph was also living beyond her means. Now it was she who needed a new loan and who was asking Winston to secure it against part of his future inheritance. The tables had turned, but Winston recognized that they were kindred spirits, 'equally thoughtless – spendthrift and extravagant. We both know what is good – and we both like to have it.' Her spending £200 on a new ball dress was no different from him spending £100 on a new polo pony (£100 in the 1890s being equivalent to thousands today).

To Churchill, 'The pinch of the whole matter is we are damned poor', though their poverty was relative. By the standards of most of the population of the world, the Churchills were rich. But not as wealthy as they had been or needed to be in order to maintain their place at the very top of British high society. Churchill was clearly worried but still confident in his own abilities to supplement his income. Another adventure was needed.

11: from Winston to Lady Randolph, 28 January 1898 (CHAR 28/24/30-32)

Jan. 28 1898

. . .

£17,000 is a great deal of money – about a quarter indeed of all we shall ever have in the world – under American settlement – Duke's will & Papa's property. I suppose that when you have got this big loan all right – you will be able to pay off all the minor ones and that the £17,000 will mark the limit of our liabilities. If it does not then our position seems very serious indeed.

. . .

Speaking quite frankly on the subject – there is no doubt that we are both you & I equally thoughtless – spendthrift & extravagant. We both know what is good – and we both like to have it. Arrangements for paying are left to the future. My extravagances are on a smaller scale than yours. I take no credit to myself in this matter as you have kept up the house & have had to maintain a position in London. At the same time we shall v[er]y soon come to the end of our tether – unless a considerable change comes over our fortunes and dispositions.

As long as I am dead sure & certain of an ultimate £1,000 a year – I do not much care – as I could always make money on the press – and might marry. But at the same time there would be a limit.

I rather wish you had written me a letter on the subject – to explain things to me – as I may be quite wrong in my conceptions of the affair. I hope you will not mind my writing in a candid manner. I sympathise with all your extravagances – even more than you do with mine. It seems just as suicidal to me when you spend £200 on a ball dress as it does to you when I purchase a new polo pony for £100. And yet I feel that you ought to have the dress & I the polo pony. The pinch of the whole matter is we are damned poor.

Forgive me dearest mamma – for appearing to preach. I realise acutely my own follies & unbusinesslike habits. But I may at least urge in extenuation – that they are on a much smaller scale, that I am confident in my own powers to supplement my income, & that some excuse for improvidence is furnished by the hopes of an approaching campaign.

...

Dearest Mamma – I send you my best love & do hope it will work out all right.

Ever your loving son,
Winston S. Churchill

'ALL THIS IN 120 SECONDS'

On 2 September 1898, Churchill charged with the 21st Lancers at the Battle of Omdurman. Once again, he had used his parents' political and social contacts to pull some strings and get himself transferred to the scene of the action. Inspired by a Muslim religious leader called the Mahdi, an army of Dervish tribesmen had taken control of the Sudan, killing the British hero General Gordon and threatening British interests in Egypt. Now, the Mahdi was dead and General Sir Herbert Kitchener had been sent to crush his followers. Kitchener did not like ambitious young officers who doubled as journalists, but could not stop Churchill using his family influence and getting himself to the scene of the action.

In his letter to Colonel Ian Hamilton, whom Churchill had known in India, you can sense his youthful excitement. Written while on a train, his hasty scrawl describes his role in the ensuing battle. As a scout, he was one of the first people to see and hear the huge Dervish army approaching. Then came a cavalry charge and fighting at close quarters. Churchill describes how one man in his troop fell

and was 'cut to pieces', and how he fired his pistol 'killing several –
3 for certain – 2 doubtful – one very doubtful'. The regiment took
significant losses and Churchill could have been killed or wounded.
Yet in a separate letter to his mother he confessed that 'my soul
becomes very high in such moments'.

Overall, the battle was a one-sided massacre with modern
British weaponry decimating the Dervish ranks. Churchill was
openly critical of Kitchener, especially of his treatment of the
enemy wounded, which is perhaps why he told Hamilton to
destroy the last part of his letter, which Hamilton dutifully did by
scoring it through in black ink. Kitchener was right to be wary of
Churchill's pen. The first edition of Winston's subsequent book
about the campaign, entitled *The River War*, repeated his criticisms
and condemned the general for desecrating the Mahdi's tomb.
He toned it down in subsequent editions, perhaps correctly
anticipating that their paths might cross again. They would in fact
both serve in the Cabinet at the beginning of the First World War.
Meanwhile, Churchill would serve under Hamilton in South Africa
and Hamilton would command the Allied armies in Gallipoli in
1915. It could be a small world at the top.

*12: from Winston to Colonel Sir Ian Hamilton, 16 September 1898
(BRDWV 1 / 1)*

In the train

Sudan Military Ra[ilwa]y
16[th] Sept[embe]r 1898

My dear General,

    ...

Well – all is over and the words Khalifa and Khartoum may now be
handed over to the historian – soldiers having no further use for them
... I had a patrol on 2[nd] Sept and was I think the first to see the enemy
– certainly the first to hear their bullets. Never shall I see such a sight
again, at the very least there were 40,000 men – five miles long in

lines with great lumps and squares at intervals – and I can assure you that when I heard them all shouting their war songs from my coign of vantage on the ridge of Heliograph Hill – I and my little patrol felt very lonely and though I never doubted the issue – I was in great awe.

Then they advanced and I watched them, fascinated ... Their cavalry patrols which consisted of five or six horsemen each made no attempt to drive me back and I waited until one great brigade of nearly perhaps 2000 men got to within 400 yards. I didn't realise they could shoot and thought they were all spearmen ...

[Later in the letter he describes the charge...]

Opposite me they were about 4 deep – but they all fell knocked A.O.T. [arse over tip] and we passed through without any sort of shock. One man in my troop fell. He was cut to pieces. Five or six horses were wounded by backhanders etc. ... Then we emerged into a region of scattered men and personal combats. The troop broke up and disappeared – I pulled into a trot and rode up to individuals firing my pistol in their faces and killing several – 3 for certain – 2 doubtful – one very doubtful. Then I looked round and saw the Dervish mass reforming ... Then I saw two men get down on their knees and take aim with rifles – and for the first time the danger & peril came home to me. I turned and galloped. The Squadron was reforming nearly 150y away. As I turned both shots were fired and at that close range I was grievously anxious. But I heard none of their bullets – which went Heaven knows where. So I pulled into a canter and rejoined my troop – having fired exactly 10 shots & emptied my pistol – but without a hair of my horse or a stitch of my clothing being touched – very few can say the same.

... It was I suppose the most dangerous 2 minutes I shall live to See. Out of 310 officers & men we lost – 1 officer & 20 men killed – 4 officers & 45 men wounded and 119 horses of which – 56 were bullet wounds. All this in 120 seconds!

...

I am in great disfavour with the authorities here. Kitchener was furious with Sir E. Wood for sending me out and expressed himself freely. My remarks on the treatment of the wounded – again disgraceful – were reported to him and generally things have been a little unpleasant. He is a great general but he has yet to be accused of being a great gentleman. It is hard to throw Stones at the rising sun and my personal dislike may have warped my judgement – but if I am not blinded – He has been on a certainty from start to finish and has had the devils [sic] luck to help him beside.

. . .

Please regard this matter as between ourselves and destroy such part of this letter as refers to it.

Hoping to see you at the end of the month.

Believe me

Yours very sincerely

Winston S. Churchill

. . .

IN SOUTH AFRICA WORKING AS A WAR CORRESPONDENT DURING
THE SECOND BOER WAR, 1900.

'I DO NOT CONSIDER THAT YOUR GOVERNMENT WAS JUSTIFIED IN HOLDING ME'

The top was where Churchill was determined to get. In 1899, he left the army in the hope of being elected as a Member of Parliament for Oldham, but lost the by-election in July, suffering the first major setback in his early career. Fortunately, the *Morning Post* newspaper was prepared to pay him handsomely for his services as a war correspondent, covering the conflict in South Africa between the Dutch Boer Republics and the British Empire.

His new adventure nearly ended in disaster. The armoured train on which he was travelling up to the frontline was ambushed and, after a defence in which, though nominally a non-combatant, Churchill clearly played a role (helping the engine to escape with the wounded), he was captured by the enemy. Some felt that as a war correspondent who had taken part in a military action, he was lucky not to be executed. That was not how Churchill saw it. Transferred to a makeshift prison in the Model States School in Pretoria he spent his twenty-fifth birthday in captivity and hated it, later writing, 'How unhappy is that poor man who loses his liberty! ... Before I had been an hour in captivity I resolved to escape.'

Escape he did, jumping over the wall and then onto a passing goods train. The letter reproduced here was left for his jailers to find and was written to Louis de Souza, the Boer Secretary of State for War. A £25 reward was issued for his recapture along with a description of him as an: 'Englishman, 25 years of age, about 5 feet 8 inches in height, medium build, stooping gait, fair complexion, reddish brown hair, almost invisible slight moustache, speaks through his nose, cannot give full expression to the letter 's', and does not know a word of Dutch.'

Despite these impediments, and after hiding in a mine, Winston reached safety in Lourenco Marques and immediately cabled de Souza, graciously informing him that his escape was no fault of the guards. Needless to say, Churchill did not rest there. By the end of his short boat journey to Durban, he had already produced his first written account of his great escape. Its publication helped make him an international celebrity and a famous Churchill in his own right. He could now enter politics.

13: from Winston to Louis de Souza, 11 December 1899 (WCHL 2 / 12)

Dec. 11th 1899
State Schools Prison
Pretoria

Dear Mr. de Souza,

I do not consider that your Government was justified in holding me, a press correspondent and a non combatant, as a prisoner, and I have consequently resolved to escape. The arrangements I have succeeded in making in conjunction with my friends outside are such as give me every confidence. But I wish in leaving you thus hastily & unceremoniously to once more place on record my appreciation of the kindness which has been shown me and the other prisoners by you, by the commandant and by Dr. Gunning and my admiration of the chivalrous and humane character of the Republican forces. My views on the general question of the war remain unchanged, but I shall always retain a feeling of high respect for the several classes of the burghers I have met and, on reaching the British lines I will set forth a truthful & impartial account of my experiences in Praetoria. In conclusion, I desire to express my obligations to you, and to hope that when this most grievous and unhappy war shall have come to an end, a state of affairs may be created which shall preserve at once the national pride of the Boers and the security of the British and put a final stop to the rivalry & enmity of both races. Regretting that circumstances have not permitted me to bid you a personal farewell, Believe me

Yours v[er]y sincerely
Winston S. Churchill

**WANTED, DEAD OR ALIVE: CHURCHILL THE ESCAPEE
PRISONER OF WAR, 1899.**

CHAPTER THREE

PUTTING DOWN ROOTS (1900–1914)

'MY PLACE IS HERE'

Churchill's formative years were dominated by army life and war. But what about romance? While in India, he had met Pamela Plowden, the daughter of the senior British official in Hyderabad, whom he described to his mother as 'the most beautiful girl I have ever known'. He carried her image into battle in South Africa in his wallet (alongside his mother's). In his letters to Pamela, he talked of his love being 'deep and strong', daring to dream of marriage, while also recognizing that there were significant obstacles. One was his lack of money. Another the fact that she had other suitors. A third was his unwillingness to compromise.

After his escape, he had rejoined the British army and was still single-mindedly seeking fame and fortune in South Africa. The letter to Pamela featured here is all about him. It is not a conventional love letter. He writes about the dangers he has been experiencing, and the horrors he has witnessed at Spion Kop (where the Boers had inflicted huge losses on the British), but argues that he cannot return home without forfeiting his self-respect and that his 'place is here'. He laments that Pamela has not travelled to South Africa with his mother, who had organized the hospital ship the *Maine*, and his brother Jack, who was coming out to fight (and would shortly be wounded). Yet his letter gives her little real romantic encouragement to do so.

One consistent feature of Winston's letters to or about Pamela are his descriptions of her as clever or wise as well as beautiful. He was clearly looking for brains as well as beauty.

1 : from Winston to Pamela Plowden, 28 January 1900 (James Drake Collection)

Government House
Natal
28 Jan. [19]00

Pamela,

Five of your letters have reached me at intervals during the last week and amid changing scenes and continual chances they were soothing & cheering. We have had as you know by now, as perhaps I hinted in my last, another serious reverse: having lost some 70 officers & 1500 men to little purpose. But I always have said, Do not be discouraged. Nothing that can happen in Natal can alter the ultimate result: Nothing that can happen anywhere except in England can prevent our final victory: though if the killing goes on at this rate I wonder who will be left to see it.

I had five very dangerous days continually under shell & rifle fire and once the feather in my hat was cut through by a bullet. But – in the end I came serenely through. I am anxious about Jack however, as I have taken a v[er]y great responsibility in bringing him out and had hoped that the relief of Ladysmith would be over before he came – but now we have the bloodiest fight of the war immediately before us – a supreme effort to break through the Boer lines. We are but grains of sand in the waves of the sea. What can we do but what we think is for the widest form of best?

I read with particular attention your letter advising and urging me to come home. But surely you could not imagine that it would be possible for me to leave the scene of war until all is over. I have joined the South African Light Horse as a Lieutenant and with them I shall serve until peace is declared or unless I get some other military appointment. But even were I only a correspondent I could not travel homewards now. For good or ill. I am committed and I am content. I do not know whether I shall see the end or not, but I am quite certain that I will not leave Africa until the matter is settled. I should forfeit my self respect forever if I tried to shield myself like that behind an easily obtained reputation for courage. No possible advantage politically could compensate – besides believe me none would result. My place is here: here I stay – perhaps forever.

My mother and Jack arrive today at Durban in the <u>Maine</u>: Oh why did you not come out as secretary? I have taken three days leave to come and meet them – one gleam of safety – and then more war – but please don't think I am not happy because I am really enjoying myself immensely and if I live I shall look back with much pleasure upon all this. I am sure I am doing what is right from the largest point of view and am careless what may result – but I have a good belief that I am to be of more use and therefore to be spared. The main thing that disturbs me is your anxiety – though I know you are too wise to be timid.

Bimbash Stewart is v[er]y talkative and v[er]y happy. He likes being shot at and is a strange queer-tempered creature, but fearless and cool under fire.

The scenes on Spion Kop were among the strangest and most terrible I have ever witnessed. The *Maine* will take 200 shattered creatures to be nursed into life again. They have suffered fearfully in jolting waggons [sic] and lying all night on the hillside, but I think their troubles are over now.

The telegram in the M.P. [*Morning Post*] which annoys you is I suppose a Reuter: and rather stupid. Do not be too sensitive about printed matter – look at the tone of the general average – not unfriendly but I have had nothing to do with anything that has been written – and I do not care two pence what they write or say or who sneers. I am fairly satisfied with what has happened here to me. That is sufficient if you agree.

I wish I had heard Algy West make such a shameful remark about our cause. I would have dressed him down. Who is it will presume to apportion God's blessings & cursings! An old man with one foot in the grave! I should tremble. The result alone can prove upon whose arms the sun shines. Why did you not come out in the *Maine* so that I should be going to meet you now. Perhaps you are wise.

Ever your loving and devoted
Winston.

it would be possible for me to leave
the scene ^here until 'all
is over'. I have joined the
South African Light Horse
as a lieutenant and with them
I shall serve until peace is
declared or unless I get
some other military appointment.
But even were I only a
correspondent I would not turn
homewards now. For good or
ill I am committed and I am
content. I do not know whether
I shall see the end or not, but
I am quite certain that
I will not leave Africa until
the matter is settled. I should
forfeit my self respect forever
if I tried to shield myself like
that behind an easily ^obtained
reputation for courage. No

Government House
Natal

28 Jun. 00

Pamela,

Five of your letters have reached
me at intervals during the
last week and amid changing
scenes and continual chances
they were ^the soothing & cheering.
We have had as you know
by now, as perhaps I wired
in my last, another serious
reverse: having lost some 70
officers & 1500 men to little
purpose. But I always have
said. Do not be discouraged. Nothing
that can happen in Natal can
alter the ultimate result: nothing

but I have had nothing to do
with anything that has
been written — and I
do not care two pence
what they write or say
or who swears. I am ^rather ^satisfied
with what has happened
here to see. That is sufficient
if you agree.
    I wish I had heard Algy West
make such a shameful
remark about our cause. I
would have dressed him down.
Who is it will presume to
apportion God's blessings &
cursings! An old man with
one foot in the grave! I should
tremble. The result alone can prove
upon whose ^side the serve ^& ^kindness.
Why did you not come out to ^the
Manor to that I should be going ^to meet
you now. Perhaps you are wise.
Ever your loving and devoted
Winston

possible advantage politically could
compensate. Besides believe me
none would result. My place
is here: here I stay — perhaps forever.
    My mother and Jack
arrive today at Durban in the
Maine: Oh why did you not
come out as secretary? I have
taken three days leave to come
and meet them — one gleam of
safety — and then more war —
but please don't think I am
not happy because I am
really enjoying myself immensely
and if I live I shall look
back with much pleasure
upon all this. I am sure

SKETCH OF PAMELA PLOWDEN, CHURCHILL'S FIRST LOVE, C. 1892.

'I DO NOT FEEL I WOULD BE BREAKING UP OUR HOME'

Winston was not the only Churchill whose thoughts were turning to marriage in 1900. His mother was an incredibly vibrant and dynamic woman, a great social networker, political organizer, accomplished pianist and occasional playwright and editor. Now in her forties, she was in love with George Cornwallis-West, a man who was just two weeks older than her eldest son. Like Winston she was unwilling to compromise when she wanted something and would marry George just two months after writing this letter. However, you can sense her concern about how Winston might take the news. She has been the driving force behind Churchill's early career and is now keen to reassure him that she is not abandoning him.

She seeks to deflect the issue by talking about Winston's marriage prospects. It was the trend of the time for British aristocrats to strengthen their finances by seeking wealthy American brides. Jennie was an American heiress herself, the daughter of a wealthy New York businessman, but she advises her son against such a course. All the indications are that she had married Lord Randolph for love, against the initial wishes of both sets of parents, and she argues that a marriage for money might prevent her son achieving his potential as a politician and writer. Jennie may have had in mind the example of Churchill's cousin, Sunny. He had married the incredibly wealthy Consuelo Vanderbilt in 1895 but the union was a loveless one that would end in separation and an annulment.

Winston's relationship with Pamela would continue for a while but by the end of 1900, it was over. She would go on to marry the Earl of Lytton, remaining a lifelong friend to Churchill, and would later say that, 'The first time you meet Winston, you see all his faults, and the rest of your life you spend in discovering his virtues.' He was not an easy person to live with. It would clearly take a very special type of woman.

2: from Lady Randolph to Winston, 26 May 1900 (PCHL 1/6)

26 May 1900
35a Cumberland Place

My dearest Winston

Your long letter from Bloemfontein dated May 1st has just reached me, also one from Jack from the Biggarsberg Camp. It was more than welcome as you may imagine as I had heard nothing from either of you since I've been home ...

But all my plans are vague. Sometimes I think I may marry G.W. I must not to you go over the old ground, but added to the reasons in favour of it is his extraordinary devotion to me through all these trying times & my absence. Also the fact that it is possible for him to help me in a money way in the future if not at present.

There is no doubt that you will never settle down until you have a house of your own, & in the 4 years that I have had this house you have spent about 3 months in all in it. I mention this to show you why I do not feel that I would be breaking up our home if I <u>do</u> marry.

But there are so many things against my doing it that I doubt its ever coming off. At the same time do not be too astonished if I did – you know what you are to me & how you can <u>now</u> and <u>always</u> count on me. I am intensely proud of you, & apart from this, my heart goes out to you & I understand you as no other woman ever will.

Pamela is devoted to you & if y[ou]r love has grown as hers, I have no doubt it is only a question of time for you 2 to marry – what a comfort it will be to you to settle down in comparative comfort.

I am sure you are sick of the war & its horrors – you will be able to make a decent living out of your writings, & your political career will lead you to big things. Probably if you married an heiress you would not work half so well. But you might have a chance in America, tho' I do not urge you to try. You know I am not a mercenary either for myself or you boys. More's the pity!

I long to see you & have a good talk ...

   ...

NEWLY WED MRS GEORGE CORNWALLIS-WEST, THE FORMER
LADY CHURCHILL, 1900.

'I HATE THE TORY PARTY – THEIR MEN, THEIR WORDS, & THEIR METHODS'

Churchill was elected to Parliament as a Conservative MP for the
northern borough of Oldham at his second attempt in October 1900.
He was only twenty-five. From the outset, he made it clear that he was
not going to shy away from controversy. In his first Commons speech,
he praised the bravery of the Boers fighting against the British in South
Africa and claimed that 'If I were a Boer I hope I should be fighting
in the field.' Thereafter, he vigorously opposed the increases in army
expenditure proposed by his own party (who were in power). Then,
perhaps echoing the role that his father had played years before, he
helped form a small group of young Conservative MPs who sought
to challenge their own government as much as the Liberal opposition.
Hugh Cecil, to whom this letter was written but apparently not sent,
was one of their number, and so they became known as the 'Hughligans'.

Churchill had inherited his father's views on the importance of free
trade. When the Conservative Party, influenced by Joseph Chamberlain,

began to move away from this policy, a mainstay of the Victorian period, towards the introduction of tariffs (charges on imports from overseas), Churchill felt that his position had become untenable. This issue cut across traditional party-political lines. It was the Brexit debate of its day. Instinctively, Churchill remained an 'English Liberal' in favour of free trade and social reform and it is clear from this letter that he had become completely disillusioned with the Conservative (Tory) Party. Once again, having taken a stand, he was not prepared to compromise. It was now a matter of principle. He was not prepared to feign friendship 'where no friendship exists' or 'loyalty to leaders whose downfall is desired'. Though the fact that this letter is marked 'not sent' suggests that he was not quite ready to say so in public.

Just eight months later, on 31 May 1904, he would dramatically cross the floor of the House of Commons and take a seat on the Liberal opposition benches. To the Conservatives, he was now a traitor. It was a huge gamble, but in the short term it paid off when the Liberal Party won a huge majority in the 1906 General Election. Churchill had successfully navigated his first major political crisis and now started to rise through the Liberal ranks.

A YOUNG STATESMAN, 1900.

3: from Winston to Hugh Cecil, 24 October 1903 (draft) (CHAR 2/8/105-106)

Most Private 24 Oct 1903

My dear Linky,

... I do not intend to be a 'loyal supporter' of the Unionist party or of this present administration, & I object to be so labelled ...

... But ... I am an English Liberal. I hate the Tory party their men, their words, & their methods. I feel no sort of sympathy with them – except to my own people at Oldham. I want to take up a clear practical position which masses of people can understand. I do not want to stay splitting hairs upon retaliation and contracting all sorts of embarrassing obligations ... I feel v[er]y uncomfortable about what I have said, & am not sure even of its honesty. To go on like this wavering between opposite courses, feigning friendship to a party where no friendship exists, & loyalty to leaders whose downfall is desired sickens me. Moreover from a tactical point of view it is the surest road to destruction.

... I want to be free to defend myself – and I mean to be. It is therefore my intention that before Parliament meets my separation from the Tory party and the Government shall be complete & irrevocable; & during the next session I propose to act consistently with the Liberal party. This will no doubt necessitate re-election which I shall not hesitate to face with all its chances.

It troubles me much to write all this; but I am convinced that the position you wish to take up is neither practical nor consistent. Free Trade is so essentially Liberal in its sympathies & tendencies that those who fight for it must become Liberals ...

...

Yours ever,

W

...

WINSTON AND HIS FIANCÉ, CLEMENTINE HOZIER, 1908.

'A FRANK & CLEAR-EYED FRIENDSHIP'

The year 1908 was a momentous one for Winston Churchill. It was the year he got married and became a Cabinet Minister. His political star had risen quickly after his defection from the Conservative Party. The new Liberal Prime Minister Campbell-Bannerman had made him Under-Secretary of State for the Colonies and he had developed his reputation as a speaker and writer, publishing a biography of his father. His red hair, eccentric dress sense and willingness to speak his mind made him instantly recognizable and a regular feature in the newspapers and cartoons of the day. In April 1908, Campbell-Bannerman's successor Herbert Asquith, made him a government minister, appointing him as President of the Board of Trade.

Churchill's name had been linked with a number of women, including the American actress Ethel Barrymore, but the main woman in his life was still his mother. All that was about to change.

Churchill had met Clementine Hozier once before, but had failed to impress her. Now he sat next to her at a dinner party, to which neither of them had been inclined to go, and found himself entranced with her 'intellectual quality' and strong reserves of noble sentiment'. There had clearly been a meeting of minds and Winston's first letter to Clementine, sent after their second date, expresses the hope that they will 'meet again and come to know each other better and like each other more'. Clementine was now travelling in Europe while Winston was 'kissing hands' at the Palace (a ceremony on becoming a minister) and fighting a by-election in his constituency of Manchester (also a result of his promotion as in those days all newly appointed ministers had to seek re-election).

Churchill's two April letters are full of the politics of his Manchester campaign, something Clementine would have to get used to. In the first, he is still optimistic of victory, but the second finds him philosophical in defeat. He puts the blame on the Irish Catholic vote turning against him, wary that he would not support Home Rule for Ireland, but this was also about Conservatives settling scores and there were question marks over the extent of his support for female suffrage (votes for women).

Clementine would have to get used to challenging such views. In his first letter, Churchill is critical of Lady Dorothy Howard, a prominent Liberal campaigner for women's rights, who had campaigned on his behalf, and suggests that women 'when they begin to think' are less capable of grasping the 'infinite variety and complexity of phenomena'. In his second letter, he is much more generous, describing Lady Howard as 'a wonderful woman – tireless, fearless, convinced, inflexible' who 'fought like Joan of Arc'.

The correspondence shows his virtues and faults. He was tireless in campaigning but generous in defeat, willing to accept the verdict of the voters and move on. He was a reformer but there were also clear limits to his radicalism. He was quickly offered a safe parliamentary seat in Dundee, but his views on women would now be challenged by Clementine at home and by the suffragists and suffragettes in public.

4: from Winston to Clementine Hozier, 16 April 1908 (CSCT 2/1)

16 April 1908

12 Bolton Street, W.

I am back here for a night and a day in order to 'kiss hands' on appointment, & I seize this fleeting hour of leisure to write & tell you how much I liked our long talk on Sunday, and what a comfort and pleasure it was to me to meet a girl with so much intellectual quality & such strong reserves of noble sentiment. I hope we shall meet again and come to know each other better and like each other more: and I see no reason why this should not be so ...

So far the Manchester contest has been quite Napoleonic in its openings & development. The three days I have been in the city have produced a most happy change in the spirits of my friends, & not less satisfactory adjustments of the various political forces ...

The Socialist candidate is not making much progress as he is deserted by the Labour party. He will however deprive me of a good many votes, and this is the most disquieting feature in a situation otherwise good and rapidly improving. Even with the risk that a contrary result may be proclaimed before this letter overtakes you, I must say I feel confident of a substantial success. Lady Dorothy arrived of her own accord – alone & independent. I teased her by refusing to give a decided answer about women's votes, she left at once for the North in a most obstinate temper ...

I never put too much trust in formulas & classifications. The human mind & still more human speech are v[er]y inadequate to do justice to the infinite variety & complexity of phenomena. Women so rarely realise this. When they begin to think they are so frightfully cock-sure. Now nature never deals in black or white. It is always some shade of grey. She never draws a line without smudging it. And there must be a certain element of give & play even about the most profound & assured convictions. But perhaps you will say this is only the sophistry of a political opportunist. Will you? Well I should not mind, so that you say it in a nice letter to

Yours v[er]y sincerely

Winston S. Churchill

16 Ap. 1908

12, BOLTON STREET,
W.

I am back here for a night and a day in order to 'kiss hands' on appointment, & I seize this fleeting hour of leisure to write & tell you how much I liked our long talks on Sunday, and what a comfort & pleasure it was to me to meet a girl with so much intellectual quality & such strong reserves of noble sentiment. I hope we shall meet again and come to know each other better and

5: from the same, 27 April 1908 (CSCT 2/1)

27 April 1908

I was under the dull clouds of reaction on Saturday after all the effort & excitement of that tiresome election, and my pen did not run smoothly or easily. This morning however I am again buoyant, and refreshed by a quiet & cheery Sunday here, I set myself to write you a few lines.

It was a real pleasure to me to get your letter & telegram. I am glad to think you watched the battle from afar with eye sympathetic to my fortunes. It was a v[er]y hard contest & but for those sulky Irish Catholics changing sides at the last moment under priestly pressure, the result would have been different. Now I have to begin all over again – probably another long & exhausting election. Is it not provoking!

The Liberal party is I must say a good party to fight with. Such loyalty & kindness in misfortune I never saw. I might have won them a great victory from the way they treat me. Eight or nine safe seats have been placed at my disposal already. From my own point of view indeed the election may well prove a blessing in disguise. It is an awful hindrance to anyone in my position to be always forced to fight for his life & always having to make his opinions on national politics conform to local exigencies. If I had won Manchester now, I should probably have lost it at the general election. Losing it now I shall I hope get a seat wh[ich] will make me secure for many years. Still I don't pretend not to be vexed. Defeat however consoled explained or discounted is odious. Such howls of triumph from the Tory Press; such grief of my poor friends and helpers; such injury to many important affairs. There is only one salve — everything in human power was done.

   . . .

Lady Dorothy fought like Joan of Arc before Orleans. The dirtiest slum, the roughest crowd, the ugliest street corner. She is a wonderful woman — tireless, fearless, convinced, inflexible — yet preserving all her womanliness.

How I should have liked you to have been there. You would have enjoyed it I think. We had a jolly party and it was a whirling week. Life for all its incompleteness is rather fun sometimes.

Write to me again — I am a solitary creature in the midst of crowds. Be kind to me.

Yours v[er]y sincerely

W

'I DO NOT LOVE & WILL NEVER LOVE ANY WOMAN IN THE WORLD BUT YOU'

Winston proposed to Clementine in the Rose Garden at Blenheim Palace in August 1908 and they were married a month later on the 12 September at St Margaret's Church in Westminster (next to Westminster Abbey and the Houses of Parliament). Their first child, Diana, was born the following July.

Churchill was extremely busy, travelling nationally and internationally as he played a key role, working alongside the

Liberal Chancellor David Lloyd George, in bringing in basic unemployment insurance and Labour Exchanges to help the jobless find work. By November, there was conflict brewing between the Liberals and the Conservatives over approval of the budget, with the Tory-dominated House of Lords threatening to reject it and prompt a constitutional crisis. Another General Election was likely. It was a tense time and probably meant long hours in the office away from his young bride and baby daughter.

Clementine always suffered from anxiety and the pressure must have been getting to her. Whatever doubts she voiced, they prompted this very full declaration of love from Winston. The letter ends with a little drawing of a dog, captioned 'wistful but unashamed'. This charming doodle was a visual rendering of her pet name for him. He was her 'pug' or sometimes 'pig'. She was his 'cat' or 'Kat' and it became their habit to sign off with these drawings. In later letters, the children appear as kittens before developing their own nicknames. Diana was the PK (puppy kitten) or Gold Cream Kitten, Randolph the Chum Bolly, and Sarah the Bumblebee or the Mule.

6: from Winston to Clementine, 10 November 1909 (CSCT 2/2)

10 November 1909

My darling,

...

Dearest, it worries me v[er]y much that you should seem to nurse such absolutely wild suspicions wh[ich] are so dishonouring to all the love & loyalty I bear you & will please God bear you while I breathe. They are unworthy of you & me. And they fill my mind with feelings of embarrassment to wh[ich] I have been a stranger since I was a schoolboy. I know that they originate in the fond love you have for me, and therefore they make me feel tenderly towards you & anxious always to deserve that most precious possession of my life. But at the same time they depress me & vex me – & without reason.

We do not live in a world of small intrigues, but of serious & important affairs. I could not conceive myself forming any other attachment than that to which I have fastened the happiness of my life here below.

And it offends my best nature that you should – against your true instinct – indulge small emotions & wounding doubts. You ought to trust me for I do not love & will never love any woman in the world but you and my chief desire is to link myself to you week by week by bonds which shall ever become more intimate & profound.

Beloved I kiss your memory – your sweetness & beauty have cast a glory upon my life.

You will find me always your loving & devoted husband.

[Drawing of Pug]   W

Wistful but unashamed.

'WE ARE GETTING INTO V[ER]Y GR[EA]T PERIL OVER FEMALE SUFFRAGE'

By the end of 1911 Churchill was First Lord of the Admiralty, the minister in charge of the Navy, and one of the most senior figures in Asquith's Liberal government. He had served as Home Secretary and been accused of heavy-handedness in the policing of female suffrage demonstrations. He had also been targeted by the suffragettes himself and was attacked at Bristol Temple Meads railway station by Theresa Garnett wielding a dog-whip. Campaigners for the female vote regularly made attempts to disrupt his meetings. Churchill's instincts when attacked were to fight back, leading him to famously, and perhaps unwisely, state that he would not be 'henpecked'.

This letter to fellow Liberal politician Alexander Murray is revealing of Churchill's thinking on the issue. His main fear was that it was so toxic that a vote in Parliament might bring down the Liberal government and cause a General Election, arguing that it would be 'a ridiculous tragedy ... if this strong Government & party which has made its mark in history was to go down on Petticoat politics!' He was basing his response on political calculations. He feared that, because any election on the issue would have to take place under the existing rules with an all-male electorate, there was a high chance it would result in a more hard-line Conservative government. His solution was to offer a referendum to women, to see if they wanted the vote, and then another one to men, to see if they would give it. He pledged himself to abiding by the result; his position perhaps now more influenced by political considerations than any personal animosities.

7: from Winston to Alexander Murray, 18 December 1911 (CHAR 2/53/83)

18 Dec. 1911

My dear Alick,

We are getting into v[er]y g[rea]t peril over Female Suffrage.

Be quite sure of this:- the Franchise Bill will not get through without a dissolution if it contains a clause adding 8,000,000 women to the electorate. Nor ought it to get through.

How can the P.M. honourably use the Parlt. Act to force it upon the King, when he has himself declared it to be a "disastrous mistake". In the second year of passage of this and the Home Rule Bill the Tories will demand a dissolution. Votes for women is so unpopular that by-elections will be unfavourable. The King will be entitled obviously to say to his Prime Minister, "You cannot conscientiously advise me to assent to this vast change. The Constituencies have never been consulted. No responsible Gov[ernmen]t is behind it. You do not believe in it yourself." The King will dismiss the Ministry & Parliament will be dissolved on the old Plural voting register. We shall be in confusion ourselves. With us will go down the Irish cause.

The situation wh[ich] is developing is v[er]y like the Free Trade split in the Tory party in 1903. I do not understand L.G. [Lloyd George] at all. His one hope was the referendum wh[ich] alone gave a reasonable & honourable outlet. He knew my view. And yet he has gone out of his way to rule it out at the v[er]y beginning.

He is exactly like Joe [Chamberlain] in 1903: It is with most profound regret that I watch these developments. I have been through it before. Do not I beseech you my friend underrate the danger. What a ridiculous tragedy it will be if this strong Government & party which has made its mark in history was to go down on Petticoat politics! And the last chance of Ireland – our loyal friends – squandered too! It is damnable.

No doubt you have made some deep calculations as to voting in H. of C. Please let me know what they are. But I do not think there is any safety there. If L.G. & Grey go on working themselves up, they will have to go, if female suffrage is knocked out. And the P.M.'s position will become impossible if it is put in.

The only safe & honest course is to have a referendum – first to the women to know if they want it: & then to the men to know if they will give it. I am quite willing to abide by the result.

What I cannot stand is making this prodigious change in the teeth of public opinion, & out of pure weakness.

Alexander the Great (your forerunner) said that the peoples of Asia were slaves because they were not able to pronounce the word 'NO'. Let you & me avoid their pusillanimity & their fate.

Your sincere friend,

W.

'THE STRICT OBSERVANCE OF THE GREAT TRADITIONS OF THE SEA TOWARDS WOMEN & CHILDREN REFLECTS NOTHING BUT HONOUR UPON OUR CIVILISATION'

There is a dramatic contrast in this letter of April 1912 from Churchill to Clementine. It starts with a cosy domestic account of reading Beatrix Potter's *Peter Rabbit* to his children, but ends with his reflections on the news of the terrible tragedy that had unfolded at sea three days earlier. In the early hours of 15 April, the huge new superliner RMS *Titanic* had hit an iceberg and sunk on its first Trans-Atlantic crossing. More than one and half thousand people had drowned. To Churchill the sacrifice of the men who stayed on board and allowed the women and children to escape in the lifeboats represented the 'great traditions of the sea' and reflected 'nothing but honour upon our civilization'.

His schooling and his passion for history had instilled in him a strong belief in chivalry. You can see it all the way through his life in the words he uses. In the Second World War, he would go on to compare the Royal Air Force fighter pilots to the 'Knights of the Round Table'. His ambiguity towards women campaigning for the vote derives in part from his sense that they are not demonstrating the virtues of 'womanliness', and in this letter he cannot resist a dig at 'young unmarried lady teachers who are so bitter in their sex antagonism'. Churchill's views were already becoming outdated in the Edwardian era. One of the constant tensions within his personality was that between his interest in new technology and his faith in old values. The First World War would see women working to support the war effort and winning their right to vote. As Minister for Munitions, Churchill would see at first hand the importance of their contribution.

8: from Winston to Clementine, 18 April 1912 (CSCT 2 / 5 / 8)

My darling,

I have just returned here after a flying surprise visit to see the P.K. [Puppy Kitten] put to bed at 6.30. Whom do you think I found nursing her? Eva! I greeted her quite pleasantly but she fled greatly embarrassed. When I came down stairs she had vanished. Both the chicks are well and truculent. Diana & I went through one Peter Rabbit picture book together & Randolph gurgled. You must have his tongue cut when you come home. It hampers his speech. He looks v[er]y strong & prosperous.

. . .

What good letters you write! Your description of the metallic light of the eclipse is perfectly correct. I noticed it myself. It also got much colder.

The *Titanic* disaster is the prevailing theme here. The story is a good one. The strict observance of the great traditions of the sea towards women & children reflects nothing but honour upon our civilisation. Even I hope it may mollify some of the young unmarried lady teachers who are so bitter in their sex antagonism, and think men so base & vile. They are rather snuffy about Bruce Ismay – Chairman of the line – who, it is thought – on the facts available – sh[oul]d have gone down with the ship & her crew. I cannot help feeling proud of our race & its traditions as proved by this event. Boat loads of women & children tossing on the sea – safe & sound – & the rest – Silence. Honour to their memory.

Sweet & beloved cat – wire your wishes. The yacht will be at Dover on Saturday and I am inspecting there. L[loyd]G[eorge] & Isaacs come for the Sunday.

Always your loving & devoted husband

W

PS Nanny now offers 13th July! Will you answer yes.

'I WILL NOT FLY ANY MORE'

It was the potential of new technology that led Churchill to take to the skies. The Wright brothers had flown the first aeroplane in 1903. As First Lord of the Admiralty, Churchill took a keen interest in the military applications of manned flight and sponsored the development of the Royal Naval Air Service. Always eager for adventure, he was keen to experience the thrill of flying himself and in 1913, only ten years after that first flight, he began to take lessons – much to the worry of his friends and family, and especially of Clementine who was pregnant with their third child. His friend F. E. Smith (later Lord Birkenhead) put it simply when he wrote, 'why do you do such a foolish thing as fly repeatedly? Surely it is unfair to your family, your career and your friends'.

Churchill's letters to Clementine and others from this period show that he was completely absorbed in flying. It became an obsession like polo. Only even more dangerous. The early planes were incredibly flimsy and unreliable. One of Churchill's instructors,

Captain Gilbert Wildman-Lushington, was killed in December 1913 and Churchill suffered a near miss in April 1914 when his plane developed engine failure, forcing an emergency landing.

In the end, he took the point that he was probably more useful as a living Cabinet Minister than a dead trainee pilot and in this letter to Clementine he agrees to stop. It was clearly a 'wrench' because he had almost achieved his pilot's wings. He would be awarded them much later and he would go on to help create the Royal Air Force and to become an Honorary Air Commodore. However, his focus on this new technology was about to be tested and vindicated in war.

9: from Winston to Clementine, 6 June 1914 (CSCT 2/7/11)

6.6.14

My darling one,

I will not fly any more until at any rate you have recovered from your kitten & by then or perhaps later the risks may have been greatly reduced.

This is a wrench, because I was on the verge of taking my pilot's certificate. It only needed a couple of calm mornings; & I am confident of my ability to achieve it v[er]y respectably. I sh[oul]d greatly have liked to reach this point wh[ich] w[oul]d have made a suitable moment for breaking off. But I must admit that the numerous fatalities of this year w[oul]d justify you in complaining if I continued to share the risks – as I am proud to do – of these good fellows. So I give it up decidedly for many months & perhaps forever. This is a gift – so stupidly am I made, wh[ich] costs me more than anything wh[ich] c[oul]d be bought with money. So I am v[er]y glad to lay it at your feet because I know it will rejoice & relieve your heart.

Anyhow I can feel I know a good deal about this fascinating new art. I can manage a machine with ease in the air, even with high winds, & only a little more practice in landings w[oul]d have enabled me to go up with reasonable safety alone. I have been up near 140 times, with many pilots, & all kinds of machines, so I know the difficulties, the dangers, & the joys of the air – well enough to appreciate them, & to understand all the questions of policy wh[ich] will arise in the near future.

It is curious that while I have been lucky, accidents have happened to others who have flown with me out of the natural proportion. This poor Lieutenant whose loss has disturbed your anxieties again, took me up only last week in this v[er]y machine!

You will give me some kisses and forgive me for past distresses – I am sure. Though I had no need & perhaps no right to do it – it was an important part of my life during the last 7 months, & I am sure my nerve, spirits, & my virtue were all improved by it. But at your expense my poor pussy cat! I am so sorry.

. . .

Always your loving & devoted,
Winston.

EMBARKING A SEAPLANE IN PORTSMOUTH, 1914.

CHAPTER FOUR

THE WORLD CRISIS (1914–18)

'EVERYTHING TRENDS TOWARDS CATASTROPHE AND COLLAPSE'

On 28 June 1914 Archduke Franz Ferdinand, the younger brother and heir presumptive of the Austro-Hungarian Emperor, was murdered in the streets of Sarajevo by the nineteen-year-old Gavrilo Princip. The teenager was seeking independence for Slavs living under Austro-Hungarian rule and their unity with Serbia, but his actions set in motion a web of complex military alliances that pitted Austria and Germany against Britain, France and Russia. In his book *The World Crisis*, Churchill relates how the British Cabinet was in session on 24 July 1914 discussing the problem of Ireland, and the growing demands for independence, when the Foreign Secretary Sir Edward Grey received and read out the terms of the Austrian ultimatum to Serbia. In Churchill's words: 'The parishes of Fermanagh and Tyrone faded back into the mists and squalls of Ireland, and a strange light began immediately, but by perceptible gradations, to fall and grow upon the map of Europe.'

The end of July was a time of intense crisis as the politicians of Europe sought to avert war while the military leaders began to plan for it. As First Lord of the Admiralty, Churchill was forced to do both. Leaving a pregnant Clementine and their two young children in a holiday cottage at Overstrand in Norfolk, he based himself at the Admiralty from where he fired off letters to his wife that capture the developing crisis.

On 28 July, Churchill decided not to order the dispersal of the British Fleet after a routine test mobilization and instead to place it on a war footing. Writing to Clementine at midnight, he confronted the duality in his own character, admitting that while 'everything trends towards catastrophe and collapse', he was 'interested, geared-up & happy' and that the preparations had a 'hideous fascination' for him. The truth was that he loved nothing more than to be at the heart of a crisis, fully engaged in directing great affairs. There is a wonderful juxtaposition in Churchill's letter between his description of the two black swans and their 'darling cygnet', peacefully paddling on the lake in London's St James's Park, and his decision to put 'the whole Navy into fighting trim'. Yet at 11pm on 4 August, when the British ultimatum to Germany expired and war came, Churchill was widely praised for the fact that the Fleet was ready.

1: from Winston to Clementine, 28 July 1914 (CSCT 2 / 7)

28 July 1914
Midnight

My darling One & beautiful –

Everything trends towards catastrophe & collapse. I am interested, geared-up & happy. Is it not horrible to be built like that? The preparations have a hideous fascination for me. I pray to God to forgive me for such fearful moods of levity –Yet I w[oul]d do my best for peace, & nothing w[oul]d induce me wrongfully to strike the blow – I cannot feel that we in this island are in any serious degree responsible for the wave of madness wh[ich] has swept the mind of Christendom. No one can measure the consequences. I wondered whether those stupid Kings & Emperors c[oul]d not assemble together & revivify Kingship by saving the nations from hell, but we all drift on in a kind of dull cataleptic trance. As if it was somebody else's operation!

The two black swans on St James's Park lake have a darling cygnet – grey, fluffy, precious & unique. I watched them this evening for some time as a relief from all the plans & schemes. We are putting the whole Navy into fighting trim (bar the reserve). And all seems quite sound & thorough. The sailors are thrilled and confident. Every supply is up to the prescribed standard. Everything is ready as it has never been before. And we are awake to the tips of our fingers. But war is the Unknown & the Unexpected! God guard us and our long accumulated inheritance. You know how willingly & proudly I w[oul]d risk – or give if need be – my period of existence to keep this country great & famous & prosperous & free. But the problems are v[er]y difficult. One has to try to measure the indefinite & weigh the imponderable – I feel sure however that if war comes we shall give them a good drubbing.

My darling one. This is a v[er]y good plan of ours on the telephone. You remember the Grand Guignol play! Ring me up at fixed times. But talk in parables – for they all listen.

Kiss those kittens & be loved for ever only by me

Your own

W.

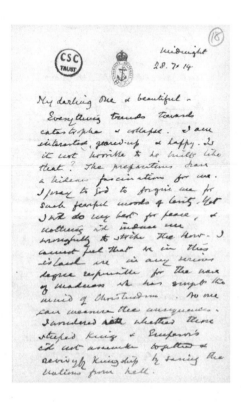

OBSERVING THE GERMAN ARMY WITH KAISER WILHELM II, 1909.

2: from the same, 31 July 1914 (CSCT 2 / 7)

31 July 1914
Secret.
Not to be left about –
but locked up or burned.

My darling –
There is still hope although the clouds are blacker & blacker. Germany is realising I think how great are the forces against her, & is trying tardily to restrain her idiot ally. We are working to

soothe Russia. But everybody is preparing swiftly for war and at any moment now the stroke may fall. We are ready.

I c[oul]d not tell you all the things I have done & the responsibilities I have taken in the last few days: but all is working well: ...

Germany has sent a proposal to us to be neutral if she promises not to take French territory nor to invade Holland – She must take French colonies & she cannot promise not to invade Belgium – wh[ich] she is by treaty bound not merely to respect but to defend. Grey [Foreign Secretary] has replied that these proposals are impossible & disgraceful. Everything points therefore to a collision on these issues. Still hope is not dead.

The city has simply broken into chaos. The world's credit system is virtually suspended. You cannot sell stocks & shares. You cannot borrow. Quite soon it will not perhaps be possible to cash a cheque. Prices of goods are rising to panic levels. Scores of poor people are made bankrupts ...

But I expect the apprehension of war hurts these interests more or as much as war itself. I look for victory if it comes.

...

I dined last night again with the P.M. Serene as ever. But he backs me well in all the necessary measures.

All the Enchantress officers on mobilisation go en bloc to Invincible. I am forcibly detaining the 2 Turkish Dreadnoughts wh[ich] are ready [for delivery]. Ireland I think is going to be settled.

...

Fondest love my darling one –
Your devoted husband
W

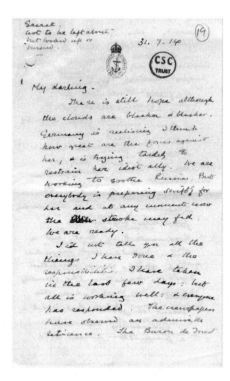

My darling –

There is still hope although the clouds are blacker & blacker. Germany is realising I think how great are the forces against her, & is trying tardily to restrain her idiot ally. We are working to soothe Russia. But everybody is preparing swiftly for her and at any moment now the stroke may fall. We are ready.

I cd not tell you all the things I have done & the responsibilities I have taken in the last few days: but all is working well: & everyone has responded. The newspapers have observed an admirable reticence. The Baron de Forest

FRONT PAGE NEWS: WINSTON'S WAR STARTED WELL.

'THE CATERPILLAR SYSTEM WOULD ENABLE TRENCHES TO BE CROSSED QUITE EASILY'

Winston Churchill had a restless drive and energy, capable of inspiring and exasperating those around him. As a member of the British Cabinet, he was not prepared to restrict his actions and interests to naval affairs, especially when the German High Seas Fleet remained in port and all the main military action was taking place on land in France and Belgium. He was eager to find outlets for himself and the British Navy, briefly taking personal command of the defences of Antwerp along with his Royal Naval Division before the city's fall in October 1914, and developing the Royal Naval Air Service. He looked for ways of attacking enemy trenches while minimizing losses and started thinking about new vehicles.

This letter to the Prime Minister, Herbert Asquith, shows his fertile mind at work. In it, he calls for the use of reinforced steam tractors as troop carriers with caterpillar tracks, supported by mobile armoured shields and the use of smoke to help screen and protect advancing Allied infantry. These ideas would lead him to establish the first experimental landships. They would become known as tanks.

Churchill did not invent the tank. What he did do was to put the resources of the Admiralty firmly behind the necessary research, becoming a leading advocate for its development. He was Minister of Munitions by the time of the first successful British tank offensive at Cambrai in November 1917 and his role as a driving force behind this new weapon was subsequently recognized by a Royal Commission on Awards to Inventors.

3: from Winston to Herbert Asquith, 5 January 1915 (CHAR 2/103/53-56)

5 January 1915
COPY.

Mr dear Prime Minister,

I entirely agree with Colonel Hankey's remarks on the subjects of special mechanical devices for taking trenches ...

The present war has revolutionised all military theories about the field of fire. The power of the rifle is so great that 100 yards is held sufficient to stop any rush, and, in order to avoid the severity of the artillery fire, trenches are often dug on the reverse slope of positions, or a short distance in the rear of villages, woods, or other obstacles. The consequence is that the war has become a short range instead of a long range war as was expected, and opposing trenches get ever closer together for mutual safety from each other's artillery fire. The question to be solved is not therefore the long attack over a carefully prepared glacis of former times, but the actual getting across of 100 or 200 yards of open space and wire entanglements ... It would be quite easy in a short time to fit up a number of steam tractors with small armoured shelters, in which men and machine guns could be placed, which would be bullet-proof. Used at night they would not be affected by artillery fire to any extent. The caterpillar system would enable trenches to be crossed quite easily, and the weight of the machine would destroy all wire entanglements. 40 or 50 of these engines prepared secretly and brought into positions at nightfall could advance quite certainly into the enemy's trenches, smashing away all the obstructions and sweeping the trenches with their machine-gun fire and with grenades thrown out of the top ...

The shield is another obvious experiment which should have been made on a considerable scale. What does it matter which is the best pattern? A large number should have been made of various patterns: some to carry, some to wear, some to wheel ...

A third device which should be used systematically and on a large scale is smoke artificially produced. It is possible to make small smoke barrels which on being lighted generate a great volume of dense black smoke which could be turned off or on at will ...

One of the most serious dangers that we are exposed to is the possibility that the Germans are acting and preparing all these surprises, and that we may at any time find ourselves exposed to some entirely new form of attack ... If the devices are to be ready by the time they are required it is indispensable that manufacture should proceed simultaneously with experiments. The worst that can happen is that a comparatively small sum of money is wasted.

'D-MN THE DARDANELLES! THEY'LL BE OUR GRAVE!'

It was the desire to use the Navy in a major offensive that led Churchill to support an ambitious plan to force the Dardanelles Straits. If ships could clear a passage into the Sea of Marmara past the Turkish forts and minefields on the Gallipoli Peninsula, they could besiege Istanbul and knock Turkey out of the war, relieving pressure on Russia and allowing her to reinforce the Eastern Front against Germany. This was the sort of grand concept that appealed to Churchill. If successful, it might shorten the war and reduce the slaughter, but it came with huge risks. The best British ships had to be held in home waters in case of a major sea battle with the German High Seas Fleet, and it was not clear that the Straits could be forced without the support of armed landings.

The debate over the Dardanelles operation became the source of increasing friction between Churchill, the civilian head of the Royal Navy, and Admiral Lord Fisher, its First Sea Lord and senior military commander. By the spring of 1915, Jackie Fisher was already seventy-four years of age. He had served as First Sea Lord between 1904 and 1910, when he had led a drive to modernize the Fleet, and had been brought back by Churchill in 1914. Like Winston, he had always been a strongly independent and divisive character. Their relationship worked while they were in agreement, but both Churchill and Fisher wanted to lead, and as differences emerged, the younger man made the mistake of trying to steamroller the older.

The breakdown in their relationship occurred in the spring of 1915 after Admiral de Robeck's failure to force the Dardanelles Straits with ships alone, suffering the loss of three battleships. This meant that military landings on the Gallipoli Peninsula were being planned and the scale of the operation was escalating, much to Fisher's dismay.

Fisher was always an eccentric correspondent, favouring quotations and multiple exclamation marks. He now warned that Churchill was eaten up with the Dardanelles and could think of nothing else, fuming 'D-mn [Damn] the Dardanelles! they'll be our grave!' Yet the note from Winston, written out dramatically in red pen just days later, captures his refusal to change course. Reciting from Shakespeare, he quotes *Hamlet*: 'And thus the native hue of resolution is sicklied o'er by the pale cast of thought', before invoking Napoleon's observation that 'We are defeated at sea because our admirals have learned where I know not that war can be made without running risks.'

Churchill's resolution was not in doubt but it blinded him to the political realities. When Fisher resigned in May, abandoning his post, Asquith had no choice but to restructure his government, bringing in the Conservatives. The price for their involvement was that Churchill (whom many of them still regarded as a traitor for his earlier defection) be removed from the Admiralty.

4: from Admiral Fisher to Winston, 5 April 1915 (CHAR 13 / 57 / 2)

5 April 1915.

Dear Winston – A.K.W. [Admiral Sir Arthur K. Wilson] spoke to me last night of the nice "kettle of fish" there'd be if those 21 fast armed German ships escaped from near York -! – Our 'Glasgow' class as he truly says no use in big Atlantic seas and heavy gales to catch these huge ships built for these seas and gales – as he says a Battle Cruiser the only thing we possess to catch them but we cant [sic] spare one! We must just chance it. From Maginness' report the Inflexible is far worse than Lion so will be quite 3 months hors de combat! The war may be over by then if Holland comes in! I don't think you are sufficiently impressed by Cambon's warning as to Holland!

<u>We ought to have every detail organized to move in a moment to Texel!</u> You are just simply eaten up with the Dardanelles and can't think of anything else! D-mn the Dardanelles! they'll be our grave! A.K.W. says Texel not Terschelling– that ought to be Settled – Kitchener ought to have some good troops told off – transports ready – every one told off! We shall be as usual "too late"! We could have had the Greeks & everyone else at the right time but we are "too late" always! This war might be described as "<u>procrastinations – vacillations – Antwerps</u>"

(that's copyright!)

Yours

F

5.4.15

ADMIRAL LORD FISHER.

5: from Winston to Admiral Fisher, 8 April 1915 (CHAR 13 / 57 / 3)

8 April 1915

"And thus the native hue of resolution

"Is sicklied o'er by the full cast of thought,

"And enterprises of great pitch & moment

"With this regard their currents turn away

"And lose the name of action"

=

We are defeated at sea because our admirals have learned, where I know not, that war can be made without running risks.

[Napoleon]

WSC

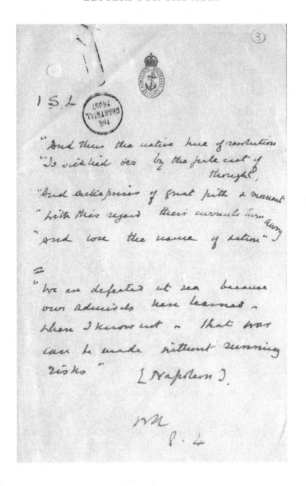

'THE DARDANELLES HAS RUN ON LIKE A GREEK TRAGEDY'

Churchill suddenly found himself demoted to Chancellor of the Duchy of Lancaster, a position without a significant department or any real power, effectively a minister without portfolio serving at the whim of the Prime Minister and facing considerable hostility from the press and public. He continued to serve on the Dardanelles Committee and looked for ways to salvage his reputation. One letter from his papers, a copy written out in the hand of his Private Secretary Eddie Marsh, shows Churchill reaching out to Admiral Sir

John Jellicoe, commander of the British Home Fleet and the most senior naval figure outside of London, in an attempt to explain the collapse of his relationship with Fisher.

According to Churchill, Jellicoe was 'the only man on either side who could lose the war in an afternoon' as the destruction of the main British Battle Fleet would be a blow from which the country might be unable to recover. As such, Jellicoe might be a useful ally in Churchill's attempts to defend his name and so he sets out all the reasons for the failure as he sees them. An interesting facet of this letter is his magnanimity towards Fisher, refusing to describe their personal separation as a quarrel and describing it instead as one of the most 'painful things' in his life.

When Churchill wrote this letter he still clung to the hope that the Gallipoli Campaign could be won. However, even as he was writing, Turkish resistance on the peninsula was proving far stronger than expected and within months the British, French, Australian and New Zealand forces would be forced to evacuate with heavy losses. Churchill was widely blamed for the defeat. His fall had been sudden and dramatic. Clementine thought he would die of grief.

The lesson Churchill took from it all was that: 'I was ruined for the time being in 1915 over the Dardanelles, and a supreme enterprise was cast away, through my trying to carry out a major and cardinal operation of war from a subordinate position. Men are ill-advised to try such ventures. The lesson had sunk into my nature.'

Next time he would make sure he was in sole charge.

6: from Winston to Admiral Sir John Jellicoe, 1 June 1915 (CHAR 2/66/51)

June 1ˢᵗ 1915

My dear Jellicoe,

My separation – quarrel there was not, from our august old friend is among the most painful things in my life. I have been looking through all the letters he wrote me, musing rightfully upon the vanished pleasures of his comradeship & society. The Dardanelles has run on like a Greek tragedy – our early successes converting what was originally launched only as an experiment into an undertaking from wh[ich] it was impossible to recede; the awful delays of the army, week after week consumed while the Germans taught the Turks to entrench, & submarines seemed ever drawing nearer; his growing anxiety when checks & losses occurred; his increasing dislike of the whole business; the imperious need to go forward to victory – you can fill in the rest. But you see it must be 'Aye' or 'No' in war.

Now the long-dreaded arrival of submarines complicates gravely the situation, & the military operation continually expands. But on the other hand the monitors [ironclad warships] are approaching, & Mr Balfour with his cool quiet courage will not leave undone any possible thing ...

I have tried not to think of myself in these days, but to keep my mind steadily fixed upon the sunny. Y[ou]r v[er]y kind letter gives me much pleasure. I hope my work here taken altogether may stand the test of after-examination. We have not always agreed as you say, but I have always felt quite safe with you at sea. Your patience inexhaustible, y[ou]r nerve untired, your practice & experience unequalled. I feel almost entitled to say the gravest & most critical period is past. In a few months anyhow when the new construction flows in all will be well – even according to y[ou]r exacting standards.

All good wishes to you in y[ou]r great command,

Yours sincerely,

Winston S. Churchill

'I AM A SPIRIT CONFIDENT OF MY RIGHTS'

Much has been written about Churchill's 'black dog' of depression, something only mentioned once by him in a letter of 1911, but what is clear is that his lowest moments came when he was no longer able to influence events. Such was the case in the summer of 1915. His sister-in-law Gwendeline introduced him to painting, and thereafter the bright colours and required concentration certainly helped to lift his spirits, but he also craved the stimulus of action. It looked briefly as though he might be able to visit Gallipoli on a fact-finding mission and observe the battle at first hand. He jumped at the chance but there were others in Cabinet who opposed his going, fearing that he might try to exceed his brief and take personal command.

This letter was written when this highly dangerous mission seemed possible and was to be sent to Clementine and opened by her in the event of his death. It illustrates his preoccupations at this time: starting with money and the need to provide for his young family, then focusing on the need to secure his Admiralty papers and through their publication restore his name and legacy, before ending with a wonderful statement of his confidence in some form of afterlife and an affirmation of his love for Clementine. The black dog is nowhere to be seen.

The Gallipoli trip did not happen and as the campaign faltered Churchill found himself excluded from the key discussions. He therefore decided to resign from the government and to take up his military commission, having remained a reservist in the Oxfordshire Yeomanry. He embarked for France while the letter presumably remained behind unopened.

7: from Winston to Clementine, 17 July 1915 (CSCT 2 / 8 / 2)
Duchy of Lancaster Office

17 July 1915

Darling,

...

The insurance policies are all kept up & every contingency is covered. You will receive £10,000 and £300 a year in addition until you succeed my mother. The £10,000 can either be used to provide interest i.e. about £450 a year or even to purchase an annuity against my mother's life, wh[ich] w[oul]d yield a much larger income at the expense of the capital. Of course it w[oul]d be much better to keep the £10,000 and live on the interest than to spend it on the chance of my mother living a long time. But you must judge.

I am anxious that you sh[oul]d get hold of all my papers, especially those wh[ich] refer to my Admiralty administration. I have appointed you my sole literary executor. Masterton Smith will help you to secure all that is necessary for a complete record. There is no hurry; but some day I sh[oul]d like the truth to be known. Randolph will carry on the lamp. Do not grieve for me too much. I am a spirit confident of my rights. Death is only an incident, & not the most important wh[ich] happens to us in this state of being. On the whole, especially since I met you my darling one I have been happy, & you have taught me how noble a womans [sic] heart can be. If there is anywhere else I shall be on the look out for you. Meanwhile look forward, feel free, rejoice in life, cherish the children, guard my memory. God bless you.

Good bye

W

A GRIM TASK: REMOVING THE DEAD FROM FIRST WORLD WAR
TRENCHES, C. 1918.

'I HAVE FOUND HAPPINESS & CONTENT SUCH AS I HAVE NOT KNOWN FOR MANY MONTHS'

Major Winston Churchill arrived in France on 18 November 1915. He was received by Sir John French, Commander-in-Chief of the British Expeditionary Force. The two men already knew and respected one another and, even though Churchill was not a professional soldier, French was prepared to offer him command of a Brigade [a unit of several thousand men comprising two or more battalions or regiments]. Churchill was set to be a Brigadier General and must have seen himself following in the footsteps of his famous ancestor, the 1st Duke of Marlborough, who had defeated the French at the Battle of Blenheim two centuries earlier. First, he needed to learn trench warfare by serving as an officer on the frontline with the 2nd Battalion Grenadier Guards.

His letters of 23 and 25 November describe his first two stints in the trenches. The vivid descriptions of the horror of the frontline, with 'graves built into the defences', 'feet & clothing breaking through the soil', 'enormous rats' and the 'venomous whining & whirring of the bullets', is offset by his obvious enjoyment and excitement at this new adventure. He is pleased that he has not lost his calmness under fire and concerned to ensure his supply of luxuries. His anger at being summoned by a general and having to walk three miles across 'sopping fields on wh[ich] stray bullets are always falling' for a meeting that does not happen is somewhat alleviated by discovering on his return that his dugout had been shelled, killing the mess orderly. If he had remained, he might well have been killed or injured. The episode causes him to reflect philosophically on the random nature of war and 'how vain it is to worry about things. It is all chance or destiny and our wayward footsteps are best planted without too much calculation. One must yield oneself simply & naturally to the mood of the game: and trust in God wh[ich] is another way of saying the same thing ...' Yet his confidence under fire hints at a belief in his own destiny and harks back to his early military adventures. Once again, he is seeking to test and prove himself in the face of adversity.

8: from Winston to Clementine, 23 November 1915 (CSCT 2/8)

23 November 1915

My darling,

We have finished our first 48 hours in the trenches & are now resting in billets in support ... I have lost all interest in the outer world and no longer worry about it or its stupid newspapers. I am living with the battalion H[ead]q[uar]ters – Colonel, 2nd in command, Adjutant. When the battalion is in the trenches, we live almost 1000 yards behind in a dugout in rear of a shattered farm ...

The neglect & idleness of the former tenants is apparent at every step. Filth & rubbish everywhere, graves built into the defences & scattered about promiscuously, feet & clothing breaking through the soil, water & muck on all sides; & about this scene in the dazzling moonlight troops of enormous rats creep & glide, to the unceasing accompaniment of rifle & machine guns & the venomous whining & whirring of the bullets wh[ich] pass over head. Amid these surroundings, aided by wet & cold, & every minor discomfort, I have found happiness & content such as I have not known for many months ...

Will you send now regularly once a week a *small* box of food to supplement the rations. Sardines, chocolate, potted meats, and other things wh[ich] may strike your fancy. Begin as soon as possible. '2nd Battalion Grenadier Guards British Exped force' is the address for this: but letters still continue to go to GHQ.

... Send me also lots of love & many kisses.

Write me all about what you are doing & what plans you are making. I enclose a note to Cox in order that you may have £100 to defray any v[er]y urgent bills wh[ich] Goonie [Gwendeline Churchill] may be troubled by. It vexes me to think she may be worried ...

Do you realize what a v[er]y important person a Major is? 99 people out of every 100 in this g[rea]t army have to touch their hats to me. With this inspiring reflection let me sign myself.

Your loving & devoted husband

W

WEARING HIS FRENCH HELMET FOR THE TRENCHES, C. 1916.

9: from the same, 25 November 1915 (CSCT 2 / 8)

[France]

25 November 1915

My Darling, I am in a dug out in the trenches. We are to be relieved tonight, thus completing our second 48-hour spell. The great & small guns are booming away on both sides but are not at the moment paying any attention to us. This morning we were shelled & I expect there will be more tonight. It has not caused us any sense of anxiety or apprehension, nor does the approach of a shell quicken my pulse or try my nerves or make me want to bob – as do so many. It is satisfactory to find that so many years of luxury have in no way impaired the tone of my system. At this game I hope I shall be as good as any. But of course we have had nothing serious yet.

Yesterday a curious thing happened ... a telegram arrived that the Corps Commander wished to see me & that a motor w[oul]d meet me at 4.30 on the main road. I thought it a rather strong order to bring me out of the trenches by daylight – a 3 miles walk across sopping fields on wh[ich] stray bullets are always falling, along tracks periodically shelled. But I assumed it was something important and anyhow I had no choice. So ... I started off just as the enemy began to shell the roads & trenches ... I just missed a whole bunch of shells wh[ich] fell on the track a hundred yards behind me, and arrived after an hour's walking muddy wet & sweating at the rendezvous where I was to meet the motor. No motor! Presently a Staff colonel turned up – saying he had lost the motor wh[ich] had been driven off by shells. He added that the general had wanted to have a talk with me but that it was only about things in general & that another day w[oul]d do equally well. I said that I was obeying an order, that I regretted having to leave the trenches at a moment when they were under bombardment, that if I was not wanted for any official duty I w[oul]d return at once. And this I did – another hour across the sopping fields now plunged in darkness ...

You may imagine how I abused to myself the complacency of this General – though no doubt kindly meant – dragging me about in rain & mud for nothing.

I reached the trenches without mishap: & then learned that a quarter of an hour after I had left, the dugout in wh[ich] I was living had been struck by a shell which burst a few feet from where I w[oul]d have been sitting, smashing the structure & killing the mess orderly who was inside. Another orderly and an officer who were inside were shaken & rattled, & all our effects buried in mud & debris. When I saw the ruin I was not so angry with the general after all. My servant too was probably saved by the fact that I took him with me to carry my coat. Now see from this how vain it is to worry about things. It is all chance or destiny and our wayward footsteps are best planted without too much calculation. One must yield oneself simply & naturally to the mood of the game: and trust in God wh[ich] is another way of saying the same thing …

… I keep watch during part of the night so that others may sleep. Last night I found a sentry asleep on his post. I frightened him dreadfully but did not charge him with the crime. He was only a lad – & I am not an officer of the regiment. The penalty is death or at least 2 years.

Will you now send me 2 bottles of my old brandy & a bottle of peach brandy. This consignment might be repeated at intervals of ten days.

We have another spell in the trenches to do before we go into Divisional Reserve to rest. After that I shall return to G.H.Q. I feel I understand the conditions and shall not be at sea if I take command. Nothing but direct personal experience as a company officer c[oul]d have given me the knowledge. Few generals have drawn their water from this deep spring.

With tender love to you and all my warmest wishes to our friends
Believe me
Your ever loving & devoted
W

'THE CRUEL POLITICS OF TODAY'
Churchill's hopes for high military command were dashed by Prime Minister Asquith who replaced French with General Sir Douglas Haig and vetoed Churchill's appointment. Winston was given command

of a Battalion of Royal Scots Fusiliers at Ploegsteert (nicknamed Plug Street) in Belgium. Churchill, who was still the Member of Parliament for the Scottish town of Dundee, threw himself into his new role. Among his officers were Archibald Sinclair, who would go on to lead the Liberal Party, and Andrew Dewar Gibb, a founder and leader of the Scottish National Party. The ordinary men were initially suspicious of this fallen Westminster politician sent to command them, and Churchill speculated that they were composed of 'Glasgow grocers, fitters, miners – all Trade Unionists probably, who I have harangued in bygone days', but he won them over with his concern for their welfare and his leadership from the front. Dewar Gibb later described one of the new commanding officer's first actions in declaring war on the lice.

Yet it is clear from these letters that Churchill's head was still in Westminster and that he could not stop playing politics. He felt betrayed by Asquith and suspicious of Lloyd George, who was clearly manoeuvring for the premiership, but he was not prepared to break with either of them and was clearly anxious to get all the latest political gossip from Clementine. His mind was already starting to plot his return.

10: from Winston to Clementine, 10 January 1916 (CSCT 2 / 9 / 12)

6th Royal Scot Fusiliers
In the field
10.1.16

My darling,

...

I continue to work at the details of my battalion wh[ich] is officered entirely by quite young boys ... they yield implicit loyalty & obedience & endeavour to meet or forestall every wish. I am fairly confident of being able to help them to do well, in spite of the woefully attentuated [sic] state of the regiment's officers.

...

I think it is rather hard lines on L.G. [Lloyd George] to be mocked at for going and facing those ill-conditioned Glasgow syndicalists. He has not played a loyal or a clever game. But still keep in touch with him. I cannot see any way in wh[ich] Asquith's interests can stand in need of me. However friendly his feelings, his <u>interests</u> are best served by my effacement. If I were killed he w[oul]d be sorry: but it w[oul]d suit his political hand. L.G. on the other hand w[oul]d not be v[er]y sorry, but it w[oul]d not suit his political hand. It is this factor that alone counts in the cruel politics of today. I can feel no sense of loyalty or friendship for Asquith after the revelation of his utter indifference shown by his letter to French. Still here again there is no occasion for a personal break.

...

Tender love my dearest one,
Your ever devoted
W
P.S. I do not ever show anything but a smiling face to the military world: a proper complete detachment & contentment. But so it is a relief to write one's heart out to you. Bear with me.

11: from the same, 13 January 1916 (CSCT 2/9/13)

In the field
13.1.16

My darling,
...

Yesterday I spent seeing all the officers & NCO's, company by company, & explaining to them how I wish things to be done. It was odd to see these politicians of a year ago – Glasgow grocers, fitters, miners – all Trade Unionists probably, who I have harangued in bygone days in the St Andrews Hall – now all transformed into Sergeants & corporals stiffened by discipline and hardened by war into a fine set of warriors.

In the morning Archie & I practised bomb-throwing. It is a job to be approached gingerly. You pull out the safety pin, & then as long as you hold the bomb in your hand nothing happens ... But the moment you throw it – or release your hand – the fuse begins to burn & then 5 seconds afterwards there is real good bang & splinters fly all over the place. As soon as you have thrown it, you bob down beyond the parapet, until the explosion has occurred. Sometimes the men are stupid – drop the bomb in the trench or close to it – then the bombing officer – a young Sandhurst kid – deftly picks it up & throws it away with perhaps 2 seconds to spare. Everyone has to learn. It is perfectly safe as long as you do it right.

...

LG by all accounts is isolated. He has been v[er]y foolish in his relations with me, Bonar Law, FE & Curzon. He might have combined us all. As it is he has earned the deep distrust of each, & I who was his friend and had worked with him so long, have now largely by his action been rendered quite powerless for the time being.

You do not tell me in y[ou]r letter what the PM said. You only say he said a lot. But I sh[oul]d like a *verbatim* report of the Kat's conversation with the old ruffian. He has handspiked compulsion as long as he c[oul]d, & long after it was needed; & only adopted it in the end against his deepest convictions, to keep his office – or what is perhaps true – to keep LG out of his office; and for this 'statecraft' at the expense of our arms & treasure – he is acclaimed as the saviour of the Nation ... However I think my time will come with him – as it did with Arthur Balfour.

...

I am going to write to Randolph. Give him & all the kittens my fondest love & many kisses.

Accept the same yourself my darling

Your ever devoted

W

'THE WAR IS A TERRIBLE SEARCHER OF CHARACTER'

Winston Churchill may have been a great orator but his speeches did not always demonstrate great political judgement. On the evening of Tuesday 7 March 1916, he used his army leave to return to the House of Commons and take part in the debate on the Naval Estimates. His criticism of government policy was going well until he made the fateful mistake of urging the recall of Admiral Lord Fisher. What he had perhaps intended as a gesture of magnanimity backfired spectacularly, reminding the assembled MPs of the breakdown between Churchill and Fisher and resulting in widespread derision in parliament.

Churchill was motivated by his desire to return to politics, and now sought permission from the Secretary of State for War, Lord Kitchener, and from Prime Minister Asquith to be allowed to leave the army. While Clementine must have been worried about the dangers of his being on the frontline, she was wise enough to see that if he returned too early it would damage his reputation. In the two letters shown here she urges caution and delay; others cannot leave the trenches and he must bide his time until he is called for; his power and prestige will recover if he waits a little longer – 'The War is a terrible searcher of character'.

This is the role that Clementine plays behind the scenes: canvassing opinion, mobilizing support and giving the 'frank & clear-eyed friendship' that Winston had called for in his very first letter to her, eight years earlier. She does not try to disguise her feelings, Winston may be prepared to forgive Fisher but she sees him as a 'malevolent engine' and is prepared to say so. When the old Admiral comes for lunch, it is Clementine who tells him to 'Keep your hands off my husband.'

12: from Clementine to Winston, 16 March 1916 (CHAR 1/118A/100-103)

March 16th (1916)
41, Cromwell Road
5.30 a.m.

My Darling

...

I am so thankful that you were inspired to send the telegram to the Prime Minister as this very grave decision needs quiet and concentrated thought which in the turmoil here it could not possibly receive. I do wish you could have seen Sir Edward Carson. I tried to give you a faithful picture in my two letters –

I think there are some solid qualities which English men and women value very highly – virtues such as steadfastness and stability – After your speech in the House of C in which you placed yourself "unreservedly at the disposal of the Military Authorities" it seems to me that more than your own conviction is needed that it is your duty to return to Parliament.

I am convinced that sooner or later the demand will be made and that once made it will become insistent. Your speech has certainly animated and vivified the Admiralty but it has done you personally harm. I mean if you had been silent or put it differently the demand for your return would perhaps come sooner. But come it will – It must.

I pray therefore my Darling Love that you may decide to bide the time. We are living on such a gigantic scale that I am sure everything ought to be simplified – our actions too, so that without explanation or justification they and their motives can be understood and grasped by all. You have assumed the yoke of your own free will like many other men, tho' none of them are in your situation. The others, having assumed the yoke cannot dis-engage themselves. You, owing to your exceptional circumstances have received the written promise of the head of the Government that in your speaking the word you shall be free. But that word must be spoken by others, if when free you are to be effective as an instrument to help the movement of events. Please forgive me my Darling if I express myself clumsily. Your old Parliamentary Secretary Mr. Whyte came to see me. He sent you affectionate messages. He is a lieutenant in the R.N.V.R. and carries Jellicoe's bags to and fro –

I have seen no-one in the official world. The last 3 days have been spent in getting back into the routine of my canteen work – Yesterday another of my restaurants was opened, for men and women making aeroplanes. The room seats only 140 and we had 190 to feed, so some of them had to stand. I made them a tiny speech – they cheered and I am sure they were all thinking of you. I long for more news of you. Write often my own Winston – I love you dearly.

    Your loving

    Clemmie

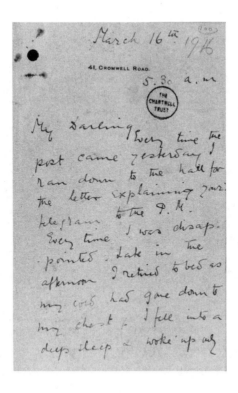

WITH THE 6TH BATTALION ROYAL SCOTS FUSILIERS, 'PLUGSTREET', 1916.

13: from the same, 24 March 1916 (CHAR 1 / 118A / 108-115)

March 24th Friday 4 a.m. [1916]
41, Cromwell Road.

My Darling

...

Sir Ian Hamilton came to tea yesterday and was very pleasant. I told him you were almost certainly coming home. He asked when? I said "I think as soon as possible; perhaps when his regiment comes out of the line" – He looked serious and said "Tell him on no account to come home before that" –

My Dearest Love you know that you can rely upon my steadfastness and loyalty, but the anxiety and grief at the step you are about to take sinks deeper into my heart day by day. It seems to me such an awful risk to take – to come back just now so lonely and unprotected with no following in the House and no backing in the country ... In your present weakened condition shall you recover prestige and the necessary power in time to be of real use? I think perhaps you may if you wait a little longer – But it is a great risk. It is indeed a gamble – If you do not succeed you may gradually decline in the public opinion ... If that happened then your return from the battlefield in the middle of the War might be a serious handicap to you in the future. The Government is nerveless and helpless but it represents all there is practically in public life. If you come back and attack them they are bound to defend themselves and try to down you. And just now you are very defenceless ... Do not be anxious about my attitude – I do not tell my thoughts to any but you. When you were here last week I did not feel that there were any great or good elements of strength surrounding you ... In the Cabinet that Judas Lloyd George never staunch in times of trial, always ready to injure secretly those with whom he is publicly associated (e.g. the sending you of those secret documents on the Naval situation was a base act of treachery to the Government, of whom he is a member. If he were honest, he would resign) … apply your mind to the future – Not only the immediate future, but the great future beyond the War of which everyone is now (perhaps it is only the hopefulness of spring-time) perceiving the dawn.

...

The atmosphere here is wicked and stifling. Out where you are it is clean and clear. I fear very much that you will be very sad and unhappy here.

...

The War is a terrible searcher of character. One must try to plod and persevere and absolutely stamp self out. If at the end one is found grimly holding onto one's simple daily round one can't have failed utterly.

...

God bless you my Darling
Clemmie

'THE PARTY OF THE FUTURE MIGHT BE FORMED'
Meanwhile, Churchill made sure that his political channels of communication remained open. His friend Frederick Smith, known as F.E., was a Conservative politician and Attorney General in Asquith's coalition government. Despite their differences of party (Churchill still being a Liberal at this point), the two men were very close. F.E. was one of the few people who could match Churchill's wit and they shared a love of good living (one that contributed to F.E.'s early death in 1930).

In the first letter, Churchill summarizes the serious military situation. Writing from the field, he describes the steady drain of men from the British front (including the deaths in his own section) and the huge losses that the French army is experiencing at Verdun. But he also has one eye on what is happening back at Westminster where he thinks the government may fall. The leading politicians of the day are identified by their initials. A is Asquith, K is Kitchener, B.L. is the Conservative leader Bonar Law and L.G. is Lloyd George. In the second letter, Churchill correctly foresees that Lloyd George and Bonar Law will be able to bring down Asquith, though this will not happen until December. You can sense his frustration at being away from the political action. He needs his friend to keep him informed and to represent his interests.

Churchill's friendship with F.E. and his openness to a new 'party of the future' is a consistent feature of his politics. He was never a party man and was always ready to enter into new combinations if they advanced his causes.

14: from Winston to Frederick (F. E.) Smith, 6 April 1916
(CHAQ 1 / 2 / 6)

6 April 1916

My dear F.E.,

...

There has now developed a good deal of Artillery fighting to the Northward, and half a mile away the wood has been heavily and persistently shelled. We are lucky and seem to be left out so far of the German operation both N and South of us. Still there is a daily toll – 7 yesterday and 3 today so far. Altogether we have lost about 100 officers and men in ten weeks out of about 500 in the trenches. I hope this drainis [sic] representative of what is taking place along the enemy's immense front.

I am in the dark completely about the g[rea]t situation; but Verdun seems to vindicate all I have ever said and written about the offensive by either side in the west. At the same time I expect the French have suffered very heavily, as division after division has been mauled by the "Cannon-Tiger" as I call the g[rea]t German heavy battery. I still think they will soon go for Russia – unless they are much weaker than we have any right to hope.

...

Yours always

W

Keep in touch with L.G. and keep him up to the mark about me.

15: from the same, 8 April 1916 (CHAQ 1 / 2 / 6)

8 April 1916
Secret.

My dear,

Probably the situation will not develop to any decisive point, in wh[ich] case I shall be able after the crisis has passed to exercise the same option that is now open to me. But if a decision is reached the result may be important for me – either way. I c[oul]d not come home <u>for</u> a crisis. Either I should have been there beforehand – wh[ich] is now impossible – or I must await the <u>coup</u> out here. This letter is the only course open to me now I must rely on you.

Generally speaking L.G. is the key to my position at the moment. However a new system might be formed, it seems to me that L.G. and I sh[oul]d be together. If he came in to what must be in substance a Tory Administration, he w[oul]d need above all Liberal associates. I think you sh[oul]d get hold of Rufus betimes and put to him v[er]y plainly the personal obligation wh[ich] exists. He has recognised it, and w[oul]d have g[rea]t weight on that point in that quarter.

I have a feeling that B.L. and L.G. have a supreme chance now, if they have the resolution to act. It does not seem material to me whether B.L. is first and L.G. war or vice versa. Either plan w[oul]d afford the basis of an effective war organisation – the easiest opening for me, tho' of course you know my wishes, if they are attainable.

The party of the future might be formed.

I am sorry the crisis comes now – if it does: but in that case it is to you I must look and do look with entire confidence that you will set my affairs first in y[ou]r thoughts. Burn this wh[ich] is for your secret eye alone.

Yours ever

W

'DEATH SEEMS AS COMMONPLACE & AS LITTLE ALARMING AS THE UNDERTAKER'

A military reorganization in May 1916 allowed Churchill to leave the army. He returned to politics but had to watch from the sidelines when Asquith's government fell in December. His old friend and rival Lloyd George became Prime Minister and in the summer of 1917 he brought Churchill back into the government, but not the Cabinet, as Minister of Munitions. Thereafter, it was Churchill's job to keep the army supplied, a complex administrative task that involved working with producers in the United States and around the world and that required regular visits to the military commanders on the frontline.

Churchill's letter of 23 February 1918 describes in graphic terms the utter devastation of the battlefields in France and Belgium. He pays a poignant return visit to 'Plug Street' and talks of the 'immense arena of slaughter', referring to the Passchendaele ridge, which had been the site of a recent battle. He refers to the fact that 'Many of our friends & my contemporaries all perished here.'

The war had been a roller-coaster ride for Churchill; high office followed by a dramatic fall leading to time on the frontline and ending with his oversight of military production. The variety of experience would ultimately serve him well in 1940, but at the time it must have been incredibly frustrating. He was conscious of the huge losses on the Western Front but his efforts to find alternative battlefields or introduce new technologies had failed or come too late.

The events of 1914–18 also changed his worldview. The devastating conflict in the European theatre was aptly described by Churchill as *The World Crisis* because it fundamentally weakened the old order. The nation states of Europe had failed to maintain the balance of power and been left in ruins. The new world in the form of the United States had been seen to come to the rescue of Britain and her allies. The dynamic of Empire had been altered: Britain was left struggling to meet the cost of direct rule in her colonies, while the dominions had gained in independence. The naval race with Germany in the years leading up to 1914, in which Churchill had played a key role as First Lord of the Admiralty, had undermined Britain's naval supremacy. The arrival of the Dreadnought, the submarine, the aeroplane and the move from coal to oil, had created a new playing field on which British dominance could no longer be guaranteed. Revolution had brought the Bolshevik communists to power in Russia, while Russian and British weakness in the Pacific had strengthened the hand of Japan. This was the aftermath of the world crisis with which Churchill was now wrestling.

16: from Winston to Clementine, 23 February 1918 (CSCT 2 / 11)

23 February 1918

My darling one,

... I went all round my old trenches at Plugstreet. Everything has been torn to pieces & the shelling is still at times severe. The British line has moved forward about a mile, but all my old farms are mere heaps of brick & mouldering sandbags. The little graveyard has been filled & then smashed up by the shells ...

...

... As for the country round & towards the enemy – there is absolutely nothing except a few tree stumps in acres of brown soil pockmarked with shell holes touching one another. This continues in every direction for 7 or 8 miles ...

CHURCHILL WATCHING TROOPS IN FRANCE, 1918.

... the view of the battlefield is remarkable. Desolation reigns on every side. Litter, mud, rusty wire & the pock marked ground. Very few soldiers to be seen mostly in 'pill boxes' captured from the industrious Hun. Overhead aeroplanes constantly fired at. The Passchendaele ridge was too far for us to reach but the whole immense arena of slaughter was visible. Nearly 800,000 of our British men have shed their blood or lost their lives here during 3½ years of unceasing conflict! Many of our friends & my contemporaries have perished here. Death seems as commonplace & as little alarming as the undertaker. Quite a natural ordinary event, wh[ich] may happen to anyone at any moment, as it happened to all these scores of thousands who lie together in this vast cemetery, ennobled & rendered forever glorious by their brave memory.

One v[er]y odd thing is the way in wh[ich] you can now walk about in full view of the enemy & in close rifle shot ... It was like walking along a street – not a scrap of cover or even camouflage. Still people kept coming and going & not a shot was fired. In my days at Plugstreet it w[oul]d have been certain death. But I suppose they are all so bored with the war, that they cannot be bothered to kill a few passers by. We on the other hand shoot every man we can see.

    ...

Your ever loving & devoted
W.

A 75-YARD SHELL CRATER, YPRES, 1917.

CHAPTER FIVE

THE EMERGING STATESMAN
(1921−39)

'THESE LAST WEEKS HAVE BEEN CRUEL'

The early 1920s were a tumultuous time for Winston Churchill and began with personal tragedy. In May 1921, his mother fell down the stairs and broke her ankle. For a while it looked as though she might recover, but infection led to amputation and then to a sudden and lethal haemorrhage. A huge and colourful presence in Churchill's life had vanished and his letter to Alfred Harmsworth (the newspaper magnate Lord Northcliffe), written two days after Jennie's death, captures something of the depth of his loss.

Yet there was more personal tragedy to come. Just weeks later, his youngest daughter Marigold, aged only two, lost her life to septicemia. Winston's papers contain newspaper cuttings and letters received relating to her death but little in his own words. It was almost certainly too personal and painful to write about.

Churchill had to contend with all this while wrestling with huge events on the world stage. As Secretary of State for the Colonies he was redrawing the map of the Middle East, creating modern-day Iraq and Jordan, and supporting Jewish immigration into Palestine. In addition, he was heavily involved in Ireland. His active support for lethal reprisals against the Irish rebels has generated much criticism, both at the time and since, though he was also instrumental in negotiating the ensuing treaty that created the Irish Free State (modern-day Ireland).

And all the while, he had to keep one eye on party politics.

1: from Winston to Lord Northcliffe, 1 July 1921 (CHAR 28/117/119)

1st July, 1921.

Mr dear Northcliffe,

Those few days at Cap d'Ail were among the last happy ones my Mother and I passed together. These last weeks have been cruel and in spite of her courage which has been amazing, their weight bore her down. We had reason and authority for hoping that the immediate dangers were warded off or surmounted, but the unsuspected end was mercifully swift.

Thank you very much for what you have written from yourself and your wife. Jack and I will miss her dreadfully. You know better than many people what a tie it is and a snap. I am also very grateful for the most dignified and honouring articles which have appeared in The Times. During these sad weeks my Mother was buoyed up by a sense of being loved and cherished by her friends and of being esteemed by the world at large. It helped her very much. Jack – I too – both feel very glad to see so much appreciation of her life and personality.

Yours very sincerely,
Winston Churchill

'I CANNOT STIR A YARD TO DEFEND MYSELF'
The British political landscape had shifted. The end of the First World War had seen the introduction of votes for all men over the age of twenty-one and for many women over the age of thirty. The Labour Party was on the rise while the Liberal Party had split. Churchill was now a 'National Liberal' serving under his old friend Prime Minister Lloyd George in a coalition government that was dominated by Conservatives. When the Conservatives pulled the plug on the coalition at a meeting in the Carlton Club, it led to the General Election of November 1922.

Churchill knew he had a fight on his hands. The Labour Party was gathering momentum in industrial heartlands like Dundee

(Churchill's constituency since 1908) while he was moving to the right and becoming an increasingly vehement opponent of socialism, which he saw as 'inspired by class jealously and the doctrines of envy, hatred and malice'. It was always going to be a struggle for him to hold his Scottish seat, but at this crucial moment his health failed him. He developed appendicitis and was too ill to campaign. He wrote this letter to his Liberal Party Association setting out his views in his absence. Clementine was spat at when she went north to campaign on his behalf and Churchill's last-minute arrival failed to stop him being defeated. He suddenly found himself 'without an office, without a seat, without a party, and without an appendix'.

For the first time since 1900, he was no longer a Member of Parliament. It must have been particularly annoying to have been replaced by Edwin Scrymgeour, the prohibitionist (anti-alcohol) candidate. It heralded the arrival of lean times in the 1920s and 30s when Churchill had to contemplate restricting his own consumption.

2: from Winston to J. C. Robertson, President of the Dundee Liberal Association, 27 October 1922 (CHAR 5/28A/20-30)

27 Oct. 1922
Colonial Office

My dear Mr Robertson

...

The situation is not one which calls for a Centre Party. I ask you to adopt me simply as a Liberal and a Free Trader; but if the public welfare requires it, I shall not hesitate to co-operate with sober, patriotic and progressive Unionist elements. These are no times when moderate-minded men can afford to dissipate friendship and support. I cannot help feeling grateful for the aid which has been accorded me with so much public spirit and disinterestedness during the last eight years by the Dundee Unionist Association. I should wish so to conduct my candidature as to make our Unionist friends feel that in supporting two Liberal candidates for the City they will be safeguarding those essential causes and principles upon which the stability of British society and the grandeur of the British Empire depend ...

And surely when we turn our eyes from this newly-fledged Administration to the formidable Socialist attack which is gathering in the opposite quarter, we must see how great is the need for patriotic men and men of sincere goodwill to stand together. We cannot afford to be divided on minor issues when the whole accumulated greatness of Britain is under challenge. A predatory and confiscatory programme fatal to the reviving prosperity of the country, inspired by class jealousy and the doctrines of envy, hatred and malice, is appropriately championed in Dundee by two candidates both of whom had to be shut up during the late war in order to prevent them further hampering the national defence ...

It is suggested that I have a special responsibility for our commitments in Mesopotamia and in Palestine, and that the leaders of the new Government are free from such responsibility. Such a suggestion is the exact contrary of to the truth. Mr Bonar Law and Lord Curzon were both members of the War Cabinet when these commitments were entered into. I was not a member of the War Cabinet, but only serving in a quasi-technical position under it ... I came into this Middle Eastern business effectively only at the beginning of 1921. At that time the joint expenditure on Mesopotamia and Palestine was nearly 45 millions a year, and Lord Curzon exercised a general control over the whole sphere of the Middle East. The Cabinet transferred these responsibilities from him to me, and in the period which has intervened I have succeeded in reducing the expenditure from its former level of 45 millions first to 30, then to eleven in the present year, and all my plans were made to reduce it to under six next year. That is my part and my only part in the affairs of Mesopotamia and Palestine. If it is now decided by Mr Bonar Law and Lord Curzon to break the promises and repudiate the obligations entered into on behalf of this country, they will be repudiating their own promises and their own obligations and not mine. But I do not think they will do anything of the sort.

Secondly, I rejoice to have been associated with the Irish Treaty settlement and to have been in charge of Irish affairs during the whole of the present year. Much of the bitterness which suddenly exploded at the Carlton Club was due to the fury of the [Conservative] Die-Hards at the Irish Treaty. This was ~~what~~ the deed they could not forgive and for which they were determined to exact vengeance. But in spite of many disappointments and difficulties and heart-breaking delays the Treaty settlement is going to live and prosper. Now that the Die-Hards have obtained office they have themselves been forced to accept our policy, and it is indeed the irony of fate that the final stages of this memorable episode should be carried out by those who have so long fomented the quarrel between the two islands and who up till a week ago were abusing in the harshest terms ~~those~~ the men who had made the peace.

During the course of the present year I have done everything in my power to sustain and defend the Government of the Irish Free State and help it along its difficult and perilous road. At the same time, however, I have been very careful to see that Ulster was put in a position to secure fully her rights and freedom of choice under the Treaty. This has been recognised by the Prime Minister of Northern Ireland during the last few days. My earnest hope is that North and South may come together as the years pass by in some form or other which they will themselves devise, and I believe that Ulster has it in her power to render in her own way and at her own time an enormous service to the British Empire.

... I have yet a word to say. In the political confusion that reigns, and with causes so precious to defend, I take my stand by Mr Lloyd George. I was his friend before he was famous. I was with him when all were at his feet. And now to-day when men who fawned upon him, who praised even his errors, who climbed into place and Parliament upon his shoulders, have cast him aside, when Wee Free fanatics think the time has come to pay off old scores, when Mr

McKenna, the political banker, emerges from his opulent seclusion to administer what he no doubt calculates is a finishing kick, I am still his friend and lieutenant. Please deal with my affairs on that basis. I am sure that among the broad masses of faithful, valiant, toiling, Britain-loving men and women whom he led to victory, there will still be found a few to wish him well.

I have to make a most melancholy confession. For the time being I am helpless. I cannot stir a yard to defend myself or the causes about which I care. I must entrust my fortunes to the Liberal Association of Dundee. All these years you have sustained me. All these years I have been your representative in the councils of the nation and indeed I may say of the Empire. Now at a moment of peculiar crisis and difficult I still rely on you. You must do with me as you please. If you decide to entrust the Liberal representation of Dundee once again into my charge you yourselves will have to organise the fight and carry it through to victory. You will have to do it almost unaided by me and in the face of many critics and traducers. But your strength and persistency of purpose has not been found wanting in the past.

I leave myself in your hands.

Yours very sincerely

Winston S. Churchill

...

'NO MORE CHAMPAGNE IS TO BE BOUGHT'

Winston Churchill first set eyes on Chartwell Manor in Kent in 1921 and immediately fell in love with it. Clementine initially shared his enthusiasm, describing it as a 'heavenly tree-crowned Hill'. Unfortunately, her views changed as she thought more about the expense of repairing, updating and maintaining this old manor house. Winston's did not and the following year he bought it without telling her. In fact, so much work was needed that it was 1924 before the family could move in. Thereafter, the house remained a source of worry and anxiety for Clementine and of joy for Winston.

He was not usually one to worry about money, preferring to live from 'pen to mouth', using his newspaper articles and books to supplement his political income and fund his lavish lifestyle. Yet, as the memorandum shown here proves, there were moments when even his optimism faded.

One of the reasons that Churchill bought Chartwell was his desire for a home within easy distance of London. He was now back in government. After two years in the political wilderness, he had been elected as the MP for Epping in Essex. The Conservatives had agreed not to oppose him and shortly thereafter he rejoined the party of his father, allegedly allowing him to remark that 'anyone could rat, but it took a certain ingenuity to re-rat'. To his surprise Prime Minister Stanley Baldwin then made him Chancellor of the Exchequer, traditionally the second post in the British Cabinet, and the office his father had briefly held in 1886.

The problem was that his ministerial salary was less than he could earn from writing while his outgoings at Chartwell remained high. The man in charge of the nation's finances was having some cash-flow issues of his own. Draconian measures were called for and putting Chartwell up for rent was considered. 'No more champagne' was to be bought, 'Cigars must be reduced to four a day' and 'No cream unless specially sanctioned'. It seems unlikely that this austerity drive lasted very long and Chartwell remained Churchill's personal escape and inspiration (and a place where there was generally plenty of champagne).

3: from Winston to Clementine, late summer 1926 (CSCT 2 / 19)

. . .

1   It is proposed first of all to put Chartwell in the Agents' hands for letting from the New Year onwards unless some very favourable offer for a long let is made. Preference will be given to a let from May till September. Every effort will be made to secure this.

All the following assumption[s] are based on a short
let next year, and a long let, perhaps, let on, if it is found
necessary:-

2 Martin [Farm Manager] leaves at Michaelmas, (September
   29th).

3 All the red poll cattle will be sold at Reading in October.
   Estimate – say – £150.

4 All the chickens and pigs, except Diana's, will be disposed
   of at the end of December.

5 All the ponies, except Energy [the last of the polo ponies]
   and her foal, will be sold as soon as any reasonable offer
   can be got …

8 During these three months the big car should be used as
   little as possible …

9 Waterhouse will be asked to look after Energy and her foal
   if the winter weather make[s] it necessary to put her in the
   stable from time to time …

10 Whatever happens about the let, neither Chartwell,
    nor Downing Street, must ever be opened for less than
    a month at a time. We must keep to this rule however
    inconvenient.

11 We had better spend the Christmas holidays in
    London, and only come down here for picnics with
    hampers …

13 The groom will leave as soon as the ponies go, or these
    holidays end, whichever is earlier.

14 <u>BILLS</u>
    Miss Street will prepare a list of £1500 of bills most
    urgent for payment in the next fortnight. All the rest,
    except a few I have ticked e.g. wine, which are running
    accounts, will be paid as soon as it is convenient to sell the
    stocks and shares. But anything pressing can be dealt with
    earlier.

    …

Nothing expensive should be bought, by either of us, without talking it over.

HOUSEHOLD EXPENSES

The Household expenses (food, wages, maintenance and car) for the last six months have averaged – say – £300, but the last two months have averaged – say – £477. We cannot afford to average more than £250 a month on these four heads ... The following should be tried at once:-

a. No more champagne is to be bought. Unless special directions are given only the white or red wine, or whisky and soda will be offered at luncheon, or dinner. The Wine Book to be shown to me every week. No more port is to be opened without special instructions.
b. Cigars must be reduced to four a day ...
c. No fruit should be ordered through the household account; but only bought and paid for by you and me on special occasions.
d. No cream unless specially sanctioned.
e. When alone we do not need fish. Two courses and a sweet should suffice for dinner and one for luncheon.
    ...
f. We must only invite visitors very rarely, if at all, other than Jack and Goonie, in September.
    The questions of reducing the household by three on our return to London must be studied, when the results of these economies are apparent.
    The cost of washing can surely be reduced, i.e. Two white shirts a week should be quite enough for me for dinner in the country ...
    There are, no doubt, many aspects of household expenses which you would like to discuss with me. I am quite ready to agree to anything that is necessary ...
    ...

'A GENERAL STRIKE IS A CHALLENGE TO THE STATE, TO THE CONSTITUTION AND TO THE NATION'

In May 1926, Britain was rocked by a general strike that threatened to bring everyday life to a standstill. It had its beginnings in the coal-mining industry, where wage cuts and worsening conditions prompted the Trades Union Congress to call for all-out collective action.

The crisis came less than nine years after the Bolshevik Revolution in Russia at a time when communist parties were on the rise across Europe, and the new Labour Party was gaining ground in Britain. Churchill's response, written to his constituency chairman after the event, clearly reveals his new-found fear of revolution. Despite having some sympathy for the plight of the miners, he sees 'Moscow influence and Moscow money' behind the general strike and opposes 'deep foreign intrigues' that are using 'sensible British workingmen' as pawns. He is at pains to draw a distinction between legitimate industrial disputes, which must be settled by negotiation, and a class war designed to challenge the State and the constitution, which must be 'fought to the bitter end'.

Not for the first or last time, Churchill waged war with words, editing a government newspaper called the *British Gazette* and helping coordinate efforts to break the strike. The episode captures a constant in Churchill's character, one that can be summarized as:

> *In War: Resolution*
> *In Defeat: Defiance*
> *In Victory: Magnanimity*
> *In Peace: Goodwill*

These were the lines that Churchill would later use to introduce his multi-volume history of *The Second World War*, presenting them as the moral of the work. They are representative of his approach to all the big issues of his life. In 1926, he was prepared to talk

with the unions before and after the general strike, but their show
of force had to be defeated. It captures his consistent approach
to opposition, equally applicable to industrial unrest at home,
independence movements in India or Nazi aggression in Europe. Yet
how much fight did Churchill have left in him?

*4: from Winston to Sir James Hawkey, 16 November 1926 (CHAR
2/147/167-173)*

16 Nov. 1926

For Sir James Hawkey.

The year that is passing away has been harassing to the
Government and deeply injurious to the nation. We have been
confronted with the most destructive industrial disturbances
which this country has experienced for generations. The fact
that the Trade Unions have become the tool of the socialist
Party has brought politics into industry in a manner hitherto
unknown in any country ... The extremists are able on nearly
every occasion to force the majority into violent courses, to
repulse all efforts at compromise and conciliation, and to levy
the class war inside the industries ~~on which the workers~~ live
[sic] in order to procure by an increase of misery the triumph
of Socialist or communist doctrines ... the miners could have
obtained seven months ago, and without suffering to themselves
or the mass of their fellow-countrymen, terms incomparably
better than those which they will now have to accept. Even three
months ago they could have had from the Government terms
greatly superior to those of which ~~they~~ their leaders have now
advised acceptance. But the Moscow influence and the Moscow
money have been powerful enough to drown the voice of reason
and good feeling ... Anyone can see the reasons for the policy
of the Russian Bolsheviks. They argue that the more miserable
and impoverished the working classes of Britain become, the
better is the chance of a bloody revolution and general collapse

which would reduce this country to the social and economical level of the Russian Republic. Beside this they saw the chance of grabbing British markets for their own coal exports. A lot of sensible British workingmen ought not to let themselves be used as pawns in these deep foreign intrigues.

There is the greatest difference between an industrial dispute, however lamentable, and a general strike. An industrial dispute about wages, hours, conditions, etc., in a particular industry ought to be settled in a spirit of compromise, with give and take on both sides. As you know, I have always tried to bring about a friendly settlement in industrial disputes. But a general strike is a challenge to the State, to the Constitution and to the ~~majesty of~~ the [sic] nation. Here there is no room for compromise. Any section of citizens, however powerful or well organised, who set themselves against the commonwealth must be made to surrender unconditionally ...

... As long as the Trade Unions confine themselves to looking after the interests of their members and of the industries out of which those members earn their wages, the issue is merely one of Labour versus Capital. But when the privileges of Trade Unions are used, not for any industrial purpose but for unconstitutional political action and to starve the public into submission, then the issue is between the citizens and the State ...

... The attempt to establish in this island a Socialist State in sympathy and alliance with Moscow will be resisted by whatever Constitutional means and measures may be found necessary ...

'MOST OF ... OUR LIVES ARE OVER NOW'
Churchill was fifty-six in 1931 and to many it looked as though his political career was over. He had ceased to be Chancellor of the Exchequer in 1929, when the Conservative government had lost to Labour, and he was increasingly at odds with the leadership of his own party over his opposition to greater independence for India. For many, the radical firebrand had become a dinosaur.

This letter suggests that Churchill may sometimes have believed this too. It finds him at his most personal, human and reflective. He writes to his old army friend Hugo Baring, with whom he had shared accommodation in Bangalore in the 1890s. His letter is a heartfelt attempt to comfort Baring on the death of his wife. He tells Hugo that he 'must dwell for a time in the good years that are gone ... Most of ... our lives are over now, & the gay memories of Bangalore seem far away. Many, many of our friends have bit the dust. The world remakes itself continually around us.'

Baring would write back acknowledging that 'It is a help in a time of desolation to have the sympathy of an old friend.' The fact that Churchill was writing from Knebworth House, the home of Lord Lytton and his wife, Winston's first love Pamela, can only have encouraged feelings of sadness and nostalgia for the vanished world of his youth. It was of course a world that he was still trying to preserve in his public life. His vehement opposition to Gandhi and those who sought independence for India in the early 1930s was grounded in views of empire developed almost 40 years earlier. They had been hardened by the losses of the First World War and by a growing sense that Britain's status as a world power was under threat. It was a campaign that had some public appeal but only limited political support. Churchill's wilderness years had begun.

5: from Winston to Hugo Baring, 8 February 1931 (WCHL ACC 2138)

8 Feb. 1931

Telephone, 10 Knebworth.

Knebworth House
Knebworth

8.2.31
Ans[were]d
13/2

My dear Hugo,

I was most deeply grieved to hear of your great loss. I offer you my heartfelt sympathy in what I know will be unendurable sorrow. You were both so devoted to each other & so happy together that life will be barren for the one who is left behind. You must dwell for a time in the good years that are gone but that still are yours to treasure. Most of both our lives are over now, & the gay memories of Bangalore seem far away. Many, many of our friends have bit the dust. The world remakes itself continually around us. We must have courage to the end.

always your friend
Winston S.C

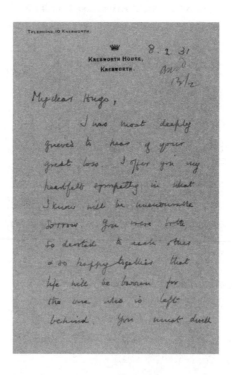

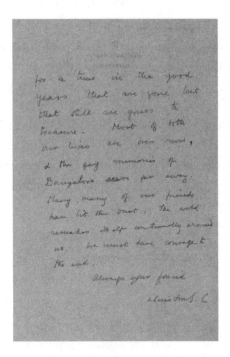

'GERMANY IS NOW THE GREATEST ARMED POWER IN EUROPE'

Everything changed with the rise of Hitler. A revived militaristic Nazi Germany, actively rearming and threatening terror and conquest, was suddenly a bigger threat to European peace and stability than Russian communism. Writing in 1935, the same year as this letter, Churchill described Hitler as a child of German 'rage and grief': a 'grim figure' cultivating a 'spirit of revenge' who had 'loosed frightful evils' and concentration camps on the Jews, socialists, communists, trade unionists, liberal intelligentsia and Christian priests. While it is true that Churchill expressed the hope that 'we may yet live to see Hitler a gentler figure in a happier age', it is impossible to read his article (subsequently published in his book *Great Contemporaries*) and believe that he thought this likely. He had identified his next opponent.

This letter is one in a series of *Chartwell Bulletins* written to Clementine. She was on a four-and-a-half-month cruise to the East Indies and Australasia, accompanying Lord Moyne on an expedition in search of a rare Komodo dragon (a type of large monitor lizard) for London Zoo. Once again, there is a tension in his text: a contrast between his 'domestic tales of peaceful England' and the storm clouds that are gathering in Germany. Faced with the defeatism of his friend and newspaper owner Lord Rothermere, Churchill states his intention to 'inculcate [create] a more robust attitude'. His campaign against the appeasement of Hitler had begun.

Churchill also describes how he is trying to adapt his speaking style to suit more modern tastes. Under the guidance of his son, Randolph, he was experimenting with a more conversational style. Thankfully, it does not seem to have taken root. It is difficult to imagine Churchill's stirring wartime speeches given in the style of one of President Roosevelt's fireside chats!

6: from Winston to Clementine, 13 April 1935 (CSCT 2 / 25)

13 April 1935

CHARTWELL BULLETIN NO. 12

There is very little to say since the last bulletin. Randolph is decisively better and only has very slight fever under 99 for a few hours in the evening each day ... He is in great good spirits and is visited by youth and beauty. He has grown a beard which makes him look to me perfectly revolting. He declares he looks like Christ. Certainly on the contrary he looks very like my poor father in the last phase of his illness. The shape of the head with the beard is almost identical.

...

The brown nanny goat named Sarah died by misadventure. Hill scattered some nitrate of ammonia on the grass. She ate it and expired. The white-horned nanny goat named Mary survived, thanks to a timely dose of castor oil. She is expecting a family.

How paltry you must consider these domestic tales of peaceful England compared to your dragons and tuataras. But I think it is very important to have animals, flowers and plants in one's life while it lasts.

. . .

At sixty I am altering my method of speaking, largely under Randolph's tuition, and now talk to the House of Commons with a garrulous unpremeditated flow. They seem delighted. But what a mystery the art of public speaking is! It all consists in my (mature) judgment of selecting three or four absolutely sound arguments and putting these in the most conversational manner possible. There is apparently nothing in the literary effect I have sought for forty years!

. . .

On the whole since you have been away the only great thing that has happened has been that Germany is now the greatest armed power in Europe. But I think the allies are all banking up against her and then I hope she will be kept in her place and not attempt to plunge into a terrible contest. Rothermere rings me up every day. His anxiety is pitiful. He thinks the Germans are all powerful and that the French are corrupt and useless, and the English hopeless and doomed. He proposes to meet this situation by grovelling to Germany. "Dear Germany, do destroy us last!" I endeavour to inculcate a more robust attitude.

. . .

More love from

W

P. S. Two black cygnets just arrived.

MAKING A SPEECH.

'LUCKILY I HAVE PLENTY OF THINGS TO DO TO KEEP ME FROM CHEWING THE CUD TOO MUCH'

One of Churchill's ways of dealing with the mounting pressure was to escape to the sun. At the end of 1935 he was installed in the luxury of the Hotel Mamounia in Marrakesh, a place that would become a favourite retreat. Here he could paint, write his biography of the 1st Duke of Marlborough and reflect on the latest political developments with old colleagues like David Lloyd George and Lord Rothermere.

The international situation was tense. Mussolini had invaded Abyssinia (Ethiopia) and a secret pact between Britain and France offering him concessions to end the conflict had just been exposed and denounced. Churchill was scathing about the British National Government, now being run by Conservative Stanley Baldwin in alliance with the former Labour Prime Minister Ramsay MacDonald. When he wrote that Baldwin was a fool not to gather Lloyd George's 'resources & experience to the public service', he was surely also thinking of his own position. He too hoped to return to the Cabinet, but this time Baldwin showed no inclination to bring him back.

The letter found him enjoying his last sip of brandy for a year. He had accepted a bet from Lord Rothermere for £600 [at least £36,000 in today's money] not to drink brandy or undiluted spirits for a year. It was a bet he would win, but he could not face the higher stakes offered for giving up alcohol altogether. 'Life would not be worth living.'

7: from Winston to Clementine, 30 December 1935 (CSCT 2/25)

30 December 1935

My darling Clemmie,

...

This is a wonderful place, and the hotel one of the best I have ever used. I have an excellent bedroom and bathroom, with a large balcony twelve foot deep, looking out on a truly remarkable panorama over the tops of orange trees and olives, and the houses and ramparts of the native Marrakech, and like a great wall, to the westward [actually eastward] the snowclad range of the Atlas Mountains – some of them are nearly fourteen thousand feet high. The light at dawn and sunset upon the snows, even at sixty miles distance, is as good as any snowscape I have ever seen.

...

I am painting a picture from the balcony, because although the native city is full of attractive spots, the crowds, the smells and the general discomfort for painting have repelled me.

...

How I wish you were here. The air is cool and fresh for we are fifteen hundred feet high, yet the sun is warm and the light brilliant ... It is much the best place I have struck so far. But the whole country is full of interest. The soil is black or red and of great fertility, plenty of water, fine harbours, everywhere excellent hotels. We must see how things go on, how far you are amused with your winter sports; how the political situation in England leaves me ...

We get excellent French newspapers and so are able to follow the French side of the political drama. There is no doubt we are in it up to our necks. Owing to this vigorous manifestation from the depths of British public opinion [against the Hoare–Laval Pact], the French have come a long way with us against Mussolini, and they will expect a similar service when the far greater peril of Hitler becomes active. We are getting into the most terrible position ... Luckily I have plenty of things to do to keep me from chewing the cud too much.

...

Rothermere offered me 2 bets. First £2,000 if I went teetotal in 1936. I refused as I think life would not be worth living, but 2,000 free of tax is nearly 3,500 & then the saving of liquor, 500 = 4,000. It was a fine offer. I have however accepted his second bet of £600 not to drink any brandy or undiluted spirits in 1936. So tonight is my last sip of brandy.

...

Tender love my darling one
from your ever loving husband
W
P.S. Many kisses to Maria [their daughter Mary].

PAINTING THE SCENERY IN MARRAKESH, 1935.

'HOW MELANCHOLY THAT WE HAVE THIS HELPLESS BALDWIN AND HIS VALETS IN ABSOLUTE POSSESSION OF ALL POWER!'

Much as Churchill enjoyed his time in the sun in Morocco, he could not escape problems at home. His hot-headed son Randolph had decided to launch his own career by contesting a by-election for the Scottish seat of Ross and Cromarty. He was not an official Conservative candidate and was standing against Malcolm MacDonald, the choice of the National Government and the son of its former leader. This was embarrassing for Winston, as it looked like a Churchill family plot and effectively quashed Winston's chances of being offered a Cabinet post. Randolph would go on to lose the election, while Churchill put the incident down to 'Kismet' or destiny.

Yet it would be the actions of the fascist powers that would really shape his destiny. Churchill was following events on the international scene very closely. His information, obtained via Lord Rothermere, suggested that Hitler was contemplating occupying the Rhineland – this was a German industrial heartland close to the French border that had been forcibly demilitarized by the Allies after the First World War. Meanwhile, Japan was occupying large parts of China. Churchill sees glimmers of hope in naval collaboration with the United States and Russia's isolation and need for Western allies but remains worried by the neglect of Britain's defences.

Perhaps it was 'kismet', or at least luck that Churchill remained in the wilderness. If he had been back in government in 1936, he could well have been implicated in what happened next. Hitler ordered his troops into the Rhineland in March. The British, French and the League of Nations took no significant action. There remained a strong public desire to avoid war and a widespread feeling that the Germans were only taking what was rightfully theirs, but the first opportunity to stop Hitler's expansion had been missed.

8: from Winston to Clementine, 15–17 January 1936 (CSCT 2/26)

15th January 1936
Hôtel Transatlantique
Meknes

My darling Clemmie,
      ...
You will no doubt have read in the papers all about Randolph. Today he telegraphs that an unimportant Scottish paper alleges I am wholeheartedly supporting his candidature. I am reluctant to disavow him and have let things drift ... I shall not make up my mind upon the matter further until I get home, but I should think that any question of my joining the Government was closed by the hostility which Randolph's campaign must excite. Kismet!
      ...

17th January.

My darling Clemmie,
      ... I think it is convenient for me to be out of England as long as possible and emphasise without ~~qualitative~~ my positive declaration ~~with~~ that I am taking no part in Randolph's campaign. The moment I return I shall be asked to say whether I approve or not ...
      ... Parliament meets on the 4th – to confront a situation which is steadily getting more difficult. Evidently there is a deep division in the Cabinet ... I fear they [the Government] have some grave news about Germany and her aggressive intentions. Certainly our Ambassador at Berlin found a very rough Hitler when he went to talk about an air pact. They are getting stronger every moment ... Rothermere who has long letters and telegrams from Hitler and is in close touch with him, believes that on the 24th or it may be the 21st, Hitler is going to make a most important announcement. This may well be that Germany will violate Article 46 and 47 of the Treaty and reoccupy the neutral zone [of the Rhineland] with troops and forts. This would immediately raise a very grave European issue, and no one can tell what would come of it. Certainly the

League of Nations would be obliged to declare the Germans guilty of 'aggression', and the French would be in the position to demand our specific aid in enforcing sanctions. So the League of Nations Union folk who have done their best to get us disarmed may find themselves confronted by terrible consequences ...

The Naval Conference has of course collapsed. Japan has ruptured it. The good thing is that we and the United States are working hand in glove and will encourage each other to strengthen the navies. Meanwhile Japan is seeking more provinces of China. Already more than half of their whole budget is spent upon armaments. Those figures I quoted about German expenditure on armaments are being admitted in the press to be only too true. One must consider these two predatory military dictatorship nations, Germany and Japan, as working in accord. No wonder the Russian bear is quaking for his sin and seeking protectors among the capitalist powers he deserted in the war, and sought to destroy at the close of it ... How melancholy that we have this helpless Baldwin and his valets in absolute possession of all power! ...

It is very nice to look forward to another week of sunshine and painting. I expect you will be surprised at my pictures when you see them. They are a cut above anything I have ever done so far. One more today! I am doing figures so much better than before. Indeed every person here however poor is a picture, & the crowds with their bright varied colours are a pageant.

My darling pussy cat – I must bring you to this place. I am sure we could spend some happy weeks here together in sunshine, when perhaps at home all was gloomy & cold.

...

Your ever devoted & loving husband
W

'A DOZEN BOTTLES OF SUNSHINE'

On returning from Marrakesh, Churchill could at least take comfort from the Christmas gift that he had received from fellow Conservative

Lord Horne: a dozen bottles of whisky to enjoy, even if the terms of his bet with Rothermere meant that he would have to drink them with water!

9: from Winston to Lord Horne of Slamannan, 27 January 1936 (CHAR 1/284/16)

27th January 1936

On returning here from some weeks of delicious sunshine in Marrakech I received the extremely gratifying intimation that you had forwarded me a dozen bottles of sunshine in an even more compendious and mobile form. A thousand thanks for this most welcome Christmas present, which I greatly appreciate in principle and will appreciate even more in practice.

Quite a lot seems to have happened while I have been away and I expect a few things more will go on happening in the near future. We must concentrate upon the defence danger.

'THIS SPANISH BUSINESS CUTS ACROSS MY THOUGHTS'

Winston would have needed a regular stiff drink as the situation in Europe continued to get worse. In the summer of 1936, General Franco led a military revolt against the Republican government in Spain and a vicious civil war ensued. Churchill was not a natural supporter of the Republicans, whom he saw as communists, later writing, 'How could I be, when if I had been a Spaniard they would have murdered me and my family and friends?'

However, he criticized the atrocities on both sides, telling the House of Commons that he would not want to 'survive in the world' under either communism or Nazism. He also knew this was a dangerous situation that could quickly escalate into a European war. He therefore urged the strict neutrality of both Britain and France (under its Prime Minister Léon Blum), writing this letter to the young Foreign Secretary Anthony Eden.

The letter is one of the first in what would become an extremely long and close working relationship between the two men. Eden would resign from the government in 1938 in protest at Prime Minister Chamberlain's refusal to take a harder line against fascist Italy. For Churchill, his departure would mark another milestone on the road towards 'drift and surrender'. It would cause Winston a sleepless night, of which he would later write, 'I watched the daylight slowly creep in through the windows, and saw before me in mental gaze the vision of death.'

Eden would ultimately serve as Churchill's Foreign Secretary from December 1940 to July 1945 and again from October 1951 to April 1955. He would also marry Winston's niece Clarissa and succeed Churchill as British Prime Minister.

The letter has been carefully prepared for post-war publication by Churchill, deleting the more personal passages at the beginning and end about the exchange of books. *Uncle, Give Us Bread* by Arne Strom was an eyewitness account of the horrors of the collectivization of Soviet agriculture. 'Twelve Days' may refer to Vita Sackville-West's account of her travels in Persia. Churchill remained an avid and very wide reader who wrote of books, 'Let them be your friends.'

10: from Winston to Anthony Eden, 7 August 1936 (CHAR 2/257/27)

7ᵗʰ August 1936

. . .

~~Many thanks for sending me "Twelve Days" which I read with pleasure. It is a very straight-forward account and obviously based on facts and experience in every line.~~

This Spanish business cuts across my thoughts. It seems to me most important to make Blum stay with us strictly neutral, even if Germany and Italy continue to back the rebels and Russia sends money to the government. If the French government take sides against the rebels it will be a god-send to the Germans and pro-Germans. In case you have a spare moment, look at my article in the Evening Standard on Monday.

~~I have ordered my bookseller to send you "Uncle, give us bread".~~ ~~I hope your rest has done you good.~~

'THE COMBINATION OF PUBLIC AND PRIVATE STRESSES IS THE HARDEST OF ALL TO ENDURE'

Churchill's focus on international issues was temporarily derailed and damaged by a new crisis in Britain. Edward VIII had succeeded to the throne, on the death of his father King George V in January 1936. The problem was that he had a mistress, Mrs Wallis Simpson, who was both an American and twice divorced, and so considered unacceptable for a Royal marriage. When the King refused to give her up, Prime Minister Baldwin, backed by the majority of the British establishment, insisted on Edward's abdication (giving up the throne).

Churchill was a long-standing Privy Counsellor (the group of senior figures who advise the sovereign) and was close to Edward. He went to see the King at the height of the crisis and tried to buy him more time, scrawling this letter to Prime Minister Baldwin and then having it typed up (presumably to allow him to write out a neater top copy).

The letter captures the King's anguished mental state, but Churchill's call for Baldwin to treat Edward with 'kindness and consideration', and not to 'extort a decision' from him, fell on deaf ears. The Prime Minister was far more in tune with the public mood on the issue than Churchill, and when Winston tried to speak in the King's defence in the Commons two days later, he was shouted down. The incident damaged his reputation and once again raised question marks over his judgement. Why did he do it? Clementine felt he was the last believer in the Divine Right of Kings, but this was also surely about chivalry and loyalty.

11: from Winston to Stanley Baldwin, 5 December 1936 (CHAR 2/264/110-113)

5 December 1936

My dear Prime Minister,

The King having told me that he had your permission to see me, I dined with His Majesty last night, and had a long talk with him. I strongly urged his staff to call in a doctor. H.M. appeared to me to be under the v[er]y greatest strain and v[er]y near breaking point. He had two marked and prolonged 'black-outs' in which he completely lost the thread of his conversation. Although he was very gallant and debonaire [sic] at the outset, this soon wore off <u>even to hardwon politeness.</u> His mental exhaustion was v[er]y painful. The combination of public and private stresses is the hardest of all to endure.

I told the King that if he appealed to you to allow him time to recover himself and to consider now that things have reached this chaos the grave issues constitutional and personal with which you have found it your duty to confront him, you would I was sure not fail in kindness and consideration. It would be most cruel and wrong to extort a decision from him in his present state.

W.S.C.

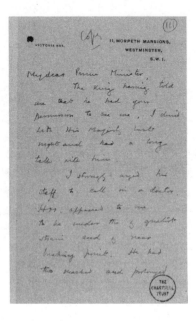

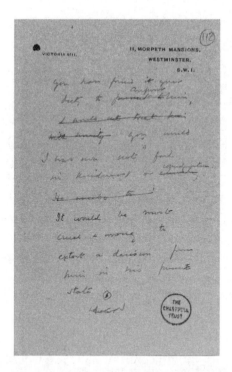

WITH SIR H. SAMUEL, LEADER OF THE LIBERAL PARTY, AT KING
GEORGE VI'S PROCLAMATION 1936.

'I THOUGHT Y[OUR] REMARK SINGULARLY UNKIND, OFFENSIVE, & UNTRUE'

Chivalry and loyalty were traits that one suspects Churchill sometimes found lacking in his own son. Randolph had inherited his father's self-belief and ability with words, but he had dropped out of university, over-indulged in drinking and gambling, and was clearly struggling to come out of Winston's shadow and find his own role. The two often clashed – loudly, though not normally for long. This particular argument seems to have occurred at a dinner where Randolph made an ill-advised joke about a gift from Churchill to Leslie Hore-Belisha (the Secretary of State for War), which had caused Churchill to lapse into a moody silence and then to write this extremely angry letter.

Randolph could be incredibly rude. His friend Evelyn Waugh once joked that when surgeons removed a benign tumour, they had managed to find the only part of Randolph that was not malignant. Yet Churchill could give as good as he got, once rebuking his son with the order, 'do not interrupt me while I'm interrupting'.

The letter reminds us that Churchill had a private life as well as a public career, and that the two would often influence one another. Clementine's trip to the Pacific, Sarah's elopement to America to marry the music hall performer Vic Oliver, the stormy arguments with Randolph, not to mention recurring financial anxieties, must all have added to the public and private stresses on Churchill during this difficult period.

12: from Winston to his son, Randolph Churchill, 14 February 1938
(CHAR 1/325/9)

14 February 1938

My dear Randolph,

I thought y[ou]r remark singularly unkind, offensive, & untrue; and I am sure no son sh[oul]d have made it to his father. Your letter in no way removes the pain it caused me, not only on my own account but on yours, and also on account of our relationship. I was about to write to you to ask you to excuse me from coming to luncheon with you on Thursday, as I really cannot run the risk of such insults being offered to me, and do not feel I want to see you at the present time.

Your loving Father,

Winston S. Churchill

A SPOT OF ROADSIDE LUNCH FOR WINSTON AND HIS SON RANDOLPH.

'I AM IN NO WAY RESPONSIBLE FOR WHAT HAS HAPPENED'

Munich – a word that is now synonymous with the failure of Prime Minister Neville Chamberlain's policy of appeasing Germany. In September 1938, having achieved union with Austria, Hitler was now demanding the return of the German Sudetenland from Czechoslovakia. War seemed imminent. At the last moment, conflict was averted when Chamberlain flew to Munich for an international summit meeting. The Czechs were given no choice but to hand the disputed territories to Germany, while Chamberlain returned with an Anglo-German agreement, which he presented as a pledge from Hitler of 'peace for our time'.

Churchill was one of the few to oppose the Munich settlement. Speaking in Parliament, he branded it 'a total and unmitigated defeat' and successfully predicted that it would lead to the rest of Czechoslovakia being engulfed by Nazi Germany. He felt the Western Democracies, Britain and France, had received a defeat without waging war and had been 'weighed in the balance and found wanting'.

Henry Page Croft was a fellow Conservative politician. He had agreed with Churchill about India and rearmament but supported the Munich Agreement as the only way of avoiding war. In this draft letter, Churchill agrees that the situation is now so serious that 'nothing can justify leading the country into defeat in war'. However, he denies that he has been advocating a preventive war and states that Britain should have sought to construct an international alliance of countries to contain Hitler. Looking forward he wants a more robust attitude against Germany from the Conservative Party and hints that he is prepared to leave its ranks to lead that fight if necessary.

It would not prove necessary. Nazi moves against the rest of Czechoslovakia would turn public and political opinion decisively behind Churchill, but they would also make war far more likely.

13: from Winston to Henry Page Croft, October or November 1938 (draft)
(CHAR 2/332/161-165)

[c. Oct. 1938]

<u>Private and Confidential</u>.

...

I agree that nothing can justify leading the country into defeat in war. War may be better than shame, but shame is better than defeat, which has a shame of its own. I submit to your sense of fair play that I have had nothing whatever to do with the policy of the course of events which led us to within an ace of war. None of the advice I gave, either on the need for preparedness or upon the conduct of foreign affairs, was taken. An opposite policy was followed, and that policy brought us, largely unprepared, to the verge of war, from which peril we escaped only at a heavy price ...

It is not true that I have advocated a preventive war. Resistance to aggression, wise or unwise, timely or not, is not a preventive war, which is in itself essentially an aggressive act designed to forestall the growing strength of an opponent. Such a war as Germany might force on us should she fear our armaments begin to overtake her, would be a preventive war. Nothing like this has been in my mind since Germany has become so strong that military operations were required. But it is true that I have used, and still use the argument that what has happened to Czechoslovakia has placed England and France at a disadvantage more substantial than anything they may recover in the next two years by development of their own forces. I need not elaborate this, because you have it all in your mind.

...

I see ~~great~~ rifts coming in the near future. It seems to me that Hitler will require of Chamberlain to have an Election before he makes his bargain, and to give proofs that he is in a position, at any rate, for several years, to 'deliver the goods.' I have no doubt where I stand in that event. It may be possible to fight within the ranks of the Conservative Party, but will there be any rally of the strong forces of the Conservative Party to defend our rights and possessions, and to make the necessary sacrifices and exertions required for our safety, or is it all to go down the drain as it did in the India business, through the influence of the Central office and the Government Whips? If so, I know my duty.

... If you tell me that our Party is definitely committed to the easy-going life, to the surrender of our possessions and interests for the sake of quietness, to putting off the evil day at all costs, and that they will go along with Chamberlain into what must inevitably be a state of subservience, if not indeed actual vassalage to Germany, and that you can do nothing to arrest this fatal tide, then I think the knowledge would simplify my course. It is for this reason that I have ventured to intrude upon you.

Yours Sincerely,
Winston S. Churchill

'CAN'T WE GET AT IT?'

By the end of August 1939, war between Britain and Germany seemed inevitable. Hitler had signed an alliance with the Soviet Union and was poised to invade Poland. Britain and France had guaranteed Polish independence. All the efforts to avoid another European war had come to nothing. Churchill was still on the backbenches, but his public profile was now high with many calling for him to be given a position in Cabinet. He was clear that the country needed to prepare for conflict, even while last-minute attempts were being made to prevent it, and he prepared this letter for Chamberlain, urging him to call up the volunteer reserves of the Territorial Army. He was no doubt recalling his role in mobilizing the Fleet in 1914. The reason that this letter was not sent was almost certainly because Churchill received his own call-up. No sooner had war been declared than Chamberlain offered him his old role as First Lord of the Admiralty. Winston was back in charge of the Navy.

Once in office, Winston wasted no time. He refused to be constrained by naval affairs and threw himself wholeheartedly into all aspects of waging war. A map room was constructed; a statistical unit was created. His Cabinet colleagues were bombarded with suggestions and questions. His letter to Samuel Hoare is typical. It explains that 'In spite of having a full day's work ... I cannot help feeling anxious about the Home Front' and then goes on to question the senseless severities of black-outs (there were not yet enemy bombing raids), restrictions on entertainment (which would damage morale) and the need for rationing. He also calls for the formation of a 'Home Guard' to take advantage of the 'vigour and experience' of the over-forties who had served in the last war, a typically Churchillian initiative and name – he would also rebrand Community Feeding Centres as 'British Restaurants'.

The final letter shown here, to the Foreign Secretary Lord Halifax, makes clear his determination to oppose any negotiation with Germany while Hitler holds any office, even ceremonial. There could be no doubt about Churchill's policy: *In War – Resolution*.

14: from Winston to Neville Chamberlain, 30 August 1939 (draft) (CHAR 2/364/25)

30, August 1939
Private.
Chartwell,
Westerham,
Kent.

My dear Prime Minister,

I think you are quite right to let things drag on, if they will; more especially because one feels a certain hesitation on the other side as the <u>act</u> approaches. But would it not be helpful to call up the reserves and mobilize the T.A. [Territorial Army]? If events turn out badly, it would prove a timely precaution. If they continue undefined, it would be an invaluable testing of machinery which is probably very rusty. Anyhow the effect would surely add to the force of your exertions to preserve peace; and the people involved would gladly respond.

I do not see myself how Hitler can escape from the pen in which he has put himself. But a victory wihtout [sic] bloodshed would be the best; and this would help, not hinder it.

Yours sincerely,
Winston S. Churchill

NEVILLE CHAMBERLAIN'S WAR CABINET, 1939.

15: from Winston to Sir Samuel Hoare, 8 October 1939 (CHAR 19/2A/51-53)

<u>PRIVATE & PERSONAL</u>   8 October 1939

My dear Sam,

In spite of having a full day's work usually here, I cannot help feeling anxious about the Home Front. You know my views about the needless and, in most parts of the country, senseless severities of these black-outs, entertainment restrictions and the rest. But what about petrol? Have the Navy failed to bring in the supplies? Are there not more supplies on the water approaching and probably arriving than would have been ordered had peace remained unbroken? I am told that very large numbers of people and a large part of the business of the country is hampered by the stinting. Surely the proper way to deal with this is to have a ration at the standard rate, and allow free purchasing, subject to a heavy tax, beyond it. People will pay for locomotion, the Revenue will benefit by the tax, more cars will come out with registration fees, and the business of the country can go forward.

Then look at these rations, all devised by the Ministry of Food to win the war. By all means have rations, but I am told that the meat ration for instance is very little better than that of Germany. Is there any need of this when the seas are open?

If we have a heavy set-back from air attack or surface attack, it might be necessary to inflict these severities. Up to the present there is no reason to suppose that the Navy has failed in bringing in the supplies, or that it will fail.

Then what about all these people of middle-age, many of whom served in the last war, who are full of vigour and experience and who are being told by tens of thousands that they are not wanted, and that there is nothing for them, except to register at the local Labour Exchange. Surely this is very foolish. Why do we not form a Home Guard of half-a-million men over forty (if they like to volunteer) and put all our elderly stars at the head and in the structure of these new formations. Let these five hundred thousand men come along and push the young and active out of all the home billets. If uniforms are lacking, a brassard would suffice, and I am assured there are plenty of rifles at any rate. I thought from what you said to me the other day that you liked this idea. If so, let us make it work.

I hear continual complaints from every quarter of the lack of organisation on the Home Front. Can't we get at it?

Yours v. sincerely,

(Sgd.) Winston S. Churchill

16: from Winston, to Lord Halifax, 1 November 1939 (CHAR 19/2A/67-68)

1 November, 1939
Private

My dear Edward,

For us to say through any channel that we could not come to terms with any Government in Germany "unless Hitler ceased to hold a position where he could influence the course of events", or words to that effect, would, by implication, mean that we were prepared to accept a government in Germany which reserved a ceremonial and honourable position for Hitler. Such an arrangement would, in my judgment, not be accepted for a moment by the British nation. We can make no arrangements with any Germany in which Hitler is an honoured figure, even though stripped of executive power. We ought not to be committed to such a position, which appears to me to be contrary to the whole basis of our public declarations and Cabinet co-operation. I was greatly disturbed that such a statement, if I understood it aright, should have been suggested. Before anything of the kind could be said, we ought to have the exact words and their context in writing, so that they could be fully discussed by the Cabinet. I cannot suppose that they would agree to it.

Generally speaking, I do not see any advantage in our dealing with German suggestions in detail. We have said that the restoration of confidence is the prerequisite of peace negotiations. It is for the Germans to establish conditions which when viewed as a whole would engender that feeling in our breasts.

There is great danger in these secret communications. If, for instance, you said anything like what you suggested, the Germans could use it to undermine French confidence in us with possibly fatal effects. On the other hand if you stand firm in accordance with our public declarations, the Germans may themselves disintegrate.

Yours sincerely,
Winston S. Churchill

THE GREAT ORATOR, 1939.

CHAPTER SIX

THE FINEST HOUR (1940–45)

'I AM UNDER NO ILLUSIONS ABOUT WHAT LIES AHEAD'
Winston Churchill became Prime Minister on 10 May 1940; the very day that Hitler launched his *blitzkrieg* offensive against France and the Low Countries. It must surely rank as one of the most dramatic days in modern British history.

Neville Chamberlain had not wanted to step down as Prime Minister. Yet it was clear that he no longer commanded the support of the Houses of Parliament. The only viable alternatives were Lord Halifax, the Foreign Secretary, who still hoped for a negotiated peace, and Winston Churchill, who believed in waging war until victory. Halifax blinked first and stepped aside.

It was already evening when Churchill returned from the Palace, having been formally appointed as Prime Minister by King George VI. He threw himself into the task of forming a new National Government. This letter to Chamberlain is one of the few that he found time to write. It shows Churchill's generosity of spirit to his defeated predecessor, but also reveals his political awareness. Chamberlain, not Churchill, remained the leader of the Conservative Party and his support for the new government was vital. He remained very popular with many Conservatives, some of whom still saw Winston as a maverick or opportunist.

Churchill finally went to bed at about 3am. He later wrote that he did so with 'a profound sense of relief' and a feeling that he was 'walking with destiny, and that all my past life had been but a preparation for this hour and for this trial'. He also knew it would be a long, hard road.

1: fromWinston to Neville Chamberlain, 10 May 1940 (CHAR 19/2C/298-299)

10.5.40

My dear Neville,

My first act on coming back from the Palace is to write and tell you how grateful I am to you for promising to stand by me and to aid the country at this extremely grievous and formidable moment. I am under no illusions about what lies ahead, and of the long dangerous defile through which we must march for many months. With your help and counsel and with the support of the great party of which you are the Leader, I trust that I shall succeed. The example which you have set of self-forgetting dignity and public spirit will govern the action of many and be an inspiration to all.

In these eight months we have worked together I am proud to have won your friendship and your confidence in increasing measure. To a very large extent I am in your hands – and I feel no fear of that. For the rest I have faith in our cause which I feel sure will not be suffered to fail among men.

I will write again to-night after I have seen the Labour leaders, I am so glad you will broadcast to our anxious people.

Believe me,

Yours ever,

(Sgd.) Winston S. Churchill.

WITH PRIME MINISTER NEVILLE CHAMBERLAIN, 1940.

'THIS HONOUR WAS DESERVED BY YOUR SUCCESSFUL EXECUTION OF A MOST DIFFICULT TASK'

Churchill may not have realized quite how difficult things would get – or how quickly. Within weeks of his becoming Prime Minister the Germans had overrun northern France and forced the Allies back to the beaches of Dunkirk.

The task of their evacuation fell to Vice-Admiral Sir Bertram Ramsay. He had come out of retirement to become the Commander-in-Chief at Dover. From his headquarters in the ancient tunnels beneath the castle, he set in motion the wheels of 'Operation Dynamo'. Over the course of ten tense days at the end of May and beginning of June, small ships, many in private ownership, supported by the might of the Royal Navy, were used to rescue over 338,000 soldiers – far more than had originally been thought possible.

This draft shows Churchill's relief at the result. His handwritten changes also show the importance of maintaining a positive message. References to 'inevitable losses' and to the numbers rescued exceeding the original 'most optimistic estimates' have been scrubbed out. It was Churchill's job to maintain morale. His speech of 4 June 1940 described Dunkirk as a 'miracle of deliverance', admitting that 'wars are not won by evacuations' but also promising to 'fight on the beaches' and pledging to 'never surrender'.

Britain and her Empire would now be fighting without their main ally. France asked for terms of surrender on the very day that Churchill wrote this letter to Ramsay.

2: from Winston to Vice-Admiral Sir Bertram Ramsay, 17 June 1940 (CHAR 2/398/3)

17 June, 1940

My dear Admiral Ramsay

I am so glad to ~~May I~~ offer you my ~~warmest~~ congratulations on your promotion to Knight Commander of the Bath. *This* ~~an~~ honour *was* ~~well merited~~ *deserved* by ~~the~~ *your* successful execution of *a most* ~~the~~ difficult task. ~~which you were called upon to carry out.~~

~~I well understand~~ The energy and foresight called for in ~~organising such a~~ so formidable an undertaking and the courage required to carry it through in ~~face~~ teeth of the ~~inevitable~~ loss ~~which were suffered.~~ *gave you full opportunity to display your qualities.*

~~The number of Allied troops landed safely in England greatly exceeded our most optimistic estimates of what was possible and bears witness to your success.~~

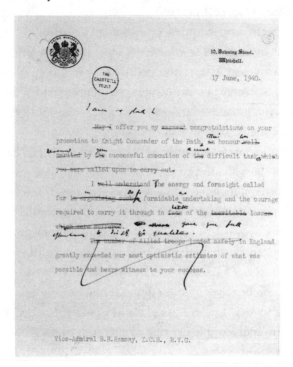

'THERE IS A DANGER OF YOUR BEING GENERALLY DISLIKED'

The Battle of France was over and the Battle of Britain was about to begin. Britain and her Empire were now fighting alone. The Soviet Union was still tied to Nazi Germany by a non-aggression pact and America was not yet in the conflict. The German Luftwaffe (air force) was on the shores of France and the United Kingdom was facing direct attack.

Churchill was under enormous pressure. At this moment, it fell to Clementine to tell the Prime Minister what nobody else could or perhaps would; namely, that he was becoming too 'rough sarcastic & overbearing' and that he had to combine 'terrific power' with 'urbanity, kindness and if possible Olympic calm'. It was a letter she clearly agonized over, setting it out once while at Chequers (the Prime Minister's country mansion), then tearing it up, before writing it out again in Downing Street.

No answer from Churchill has been found but we can be fairly certain that he listened to his 'devoted & watchful' cat. She wrote it out because she knew her husband would pay attention to a letter and she kept it as part of the historical record; as an insight into their relationship but also as an important glimpse into the pressures of leadership. The events of 1940 are often presented in a glamorous and heroic light. Yet to those who were there at the time, like Churchill's Private Secretary John Martin, they had seemed 'a time of agony piled on agony'. It cannot always have been easy for Churchill to remain so resolute and confident in public.

3: from Clementine to Winston, 27 June 1940 (CSCT 1 / 24)

27 June 1940

My Darling

I hope you will forgive me if I tell you something I feel you ought to know.

One of the men in your entourage (a devoted friend) has been to me & told me that there is a danger of your being generally disliked by your colleagues and subordinates because of your rough sarcastic & overbearing manner – It seems your Private Secretaries have agreed to behave like schoolboys & 'take what's coming to them' & then escape out of your presence shrugging their shoulders – Higher up, if an idea is suggested (say at a conference) you are supposed to be so contemptuous that presently no ideas, good or bad, will be forthcoming. I was so astonished & upset because in all these years I have been accustomed to all those who have worked with & under you, loving you – I said this & I was told 'No doubt it's the strain' –

My Darling Winston – I must confess that I have noticed a deterioration in your manner; & you are not so kind as you used to be.

It is for you to give the Orders & if they are bungled – except for the King the Archbishop of Canterbury & the Speaker [of the House of Commons] you can sack anyone & everyone – Therefore with this terrific power you must combine urbanity, kindness and if possible Olympic calm. You used to quote:- 'On ne règne sur les âmes que par le calme' [one cannot reign over hearts except by keeping calm] – I cannot bear that those who serve the Country & yourself should not love you as well as admire and respect you –

Besides you won't get the best results by irascibility & rudeness. They <u>will</u> breed either dislike or a slave mentality – (Rebellion in War time being out of the question!)

Please forgive your loving devoted & watchful
Clemmie

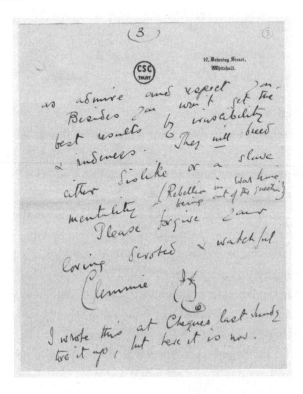

'NEVER SURRENDERING OR SCUTTLING HER FLEET'

Churchill's battle cry of 'never surrender' was directed at the President of the United States. The British military commanders had been clear that Britain could only fight on if the United States of America was willing to give 'full economic and financial support, without which we do not think we could continue the war with any chance of success'.

Franklin Roosevelt was cautious. He had decided to run for an unprecedented third term as President. American public and political opinion was still opposed to involvement in another European war, and there seemed a very real risk that money and supplies sent to Britain would be wasted if the Germans achieved victory.

The British Prime Minister and the American President struck a deal. The Americans would supply the British with fifty old naval destroyers. These would help the Royal Navy release more modern ships for frontline duties. In return, the British would give the Americans long-term leases in naval bases around the world. Roosevelt wanted an assurance that, in the event of a British defeat, the Royal Navy would sail across the Atlantic. Churchill was not prepared to send such a defeatist signal but he pledged that the Fleet would not be surrendered or scuttled. In Parliament he talked of the British Empire and the United States getting 'somewhat mixed up together' and likened greater Anglo-American cooperation to the mighty Mississippi River: 'Like the Mississippi, it just keeps rolling along. Let it roll. Let it roll on full flood, inexorable irresistible, benignant, to broader lands and better days.'

4: from Winston to President Roosevelt, 31 August 1940 (CHAR 20/1/66)

Prime Minister to President.

Your telegram No. 573, August 30

Your ask Mr. President whether my statement in Parliament on June 4 1940 about Great Britain never surrendering or scuttling her fleet, "represents the settled policy of His Majesty's Government."

It certainly does STOP I must however observe that these hypothetical contingencies are more likely to concern the German Fleet, or what is left of it than our own STOP

WITH PRESIDENT FRANKLIN D. ROOSEVELT, AUGUST 1941.

'IT'S A GRAND LIFE, IF WE DON'T WEAKEN'

Those better days would not come straight away. The 'Blitz' began on 7 September 1940, with the Germans targeting British cities. Night after night, month after month, the bombs fell. The cost in lives and property was enormous.

London was bombed for fifty-six consecutive nights (seventy-five excluding only 2 November). The war had literally arrived on Churchill's doorstep. This letter to Neville Chamberlain describes a near miss. Churchill had been dining at Downing Street on 14 October when two high-explosive bombs fell on the nearby Treasury, killing several and severely damaging No. 10. In his war memoirs, he describes how he had ordered his cook, Mrs Landemare, and her team into the air-raid shelter just minutes before the impact.

Winston and Clementine were forced to move into the Treasury Annexe, immediately above the underground command bunker, which is now the site of the Churchill War Rooms museum. Attempts to make the Prime Minister sleep below ground during air raids were largely unsuccessful. He disliked leading what he described as a 'troglodyte' existence and very rarely used his subterranean bedroom.

Chamberlain was now gravely ill and would die within weeks. Churchill could not have been more alive. Events were bringing back memories of his time commanding troops under fire in the First World War, and he clearly relished reporting the fighting spirit shown by the Home Guard volunteers. Having inspected the bomb sites, he was confident that British morale would hold and that the Germans could be worn down and defeated.

5: *from Winston to Neville Chamberlain, 20 October 1940 (CHAR 20/2A/66-67)*

20 October, 1940

My dear Neville,

I do hope you are getting on and finding relief in repose. The weeks in London have become very hard now with the press of business and our numerous meetings having to be arranged under continued Alerts and Alarms. We have had two very near misses with big H.E. [High Explosive] bombs at No. 10. They fell in the little yard by the Treasury passage, one in the corner and the other on the Treasury, the first killing one and wounding two and the second killing four, including two principal clerks serving in the Home Guard. The effect of these explosions has been to shatter all our windows, doors, etc. on the exposed side, and render the greater part of the house uninhabitable. However, the Cabinet Room is intact, and I am carrying on for the present in the downstairs rooms formerly used by the secretaries who dealt with correspondence.

... I heard one of the Home Guard remark the other night, "It's a grand life, if we don't weaken."

The Germans have made a tremendous mistake in concentrating on London to the relief of our factories, and in trying to intimidate a people whom they have only infuriated. I feel very hopeful about the future, and that we shall wear them down and break them up. But it will take a long time.

It has occured [sic] to me that while you are, I am sure, glad to be relieved of the mass of Papers which War Cabinet Ministers have had to wade through, you might like to see occasional Papers or Telegrams on some points of special interest. In case you should feel any scruple about what is, perhaps, a somewhat unorthodox arrangement, I mentioned my intention to make this arrangement to the King the other day, and he most cordially approved it. I am telling Bridges to send you occasional Papers on matters which he thinks are likely to interest you especially, without sending so much as to become a burden.

Pray give my kindest regards to Mrs. Neville,

and believe me,

Yours ever,

(Sgd.) Winston S. Churchill

P.S. Very bad news has just come in about our convoys in N.W. Approaches. But we shall be stronger there in a month or so.

(Intld.) W.S.C.

INSPECTING THE DAMAGE MADE BY A GERMAN AIR RAID IN
BATTERSEA, 1940.

'SAIL ON, O SHIP OF STATE'

But how long could Britain survive without American support? Churchill remained determined to reel in the United States, declaring that 'No lover ever studied every whim of his mistress as I did those of President Roosevelt.' Yet progress remained painfully slow. Then, in January, Roosevelt sent his trusted aide Harry Hopkins to Britain, before following up with this handwritten letter of personal support in which he quotes from the Longfellow poem 'The Sailing of the Ship'. It ends with the poignant lines, 'Humanity with all its fears, with all the hopes of future years, is hanging breathless on thy fate!'

Written at some point during Roosevelt's inauguration day, this letter marked a turning point. The choice of text was clearly designed to appeal to Churchill's romantic nature, and Winston duly had it framed and hung on his study wall at Chartwell. Yet both men knew that it was also a message of support that was intended for public release. Churchill broadcast it back across the Atlantic on 9 February 1941, asking, 'What is the answer that I shall give, in your name, to this great man ... Here is the answer which I will give to President Roosevelt ... Give us the tools, and we will finish the job.' This was diplomacy by rhetoric on the part of both leaders, aimed at bolstering British morale and moving American public opinion.

Provision for the tools duly came in the form of the American Lend-Lease Act, which was signed into law on 11 March, and which authorized the President to transfer arms and other defence materials to any country whose defence he deemed vital to the interests of the United States. A special relationship was being forged, but it would still be almost a year before America joined the conflict.

6: from President Roosevelt to Winston: 20 January 1941 (WCHL 13 / 1)
20 Jan. 1941

Dear Churchill

Wendell Willkie will give you this – He is truly helping to keep politics out over here.

I think this verse applies to your people as it does to us:

> "Sail on, O Ship of State!
> Sail on, O Union, strong and great.
> Humanity with all its fears,
> With all the hope of future years
> Is hanging breathless on thy fate."

As ever yours,
Franklin D Roosevelt

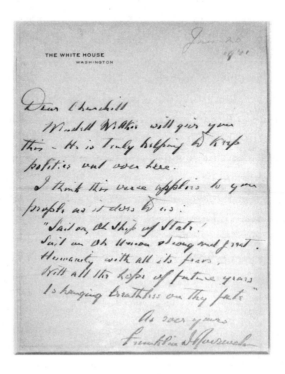

'NOW OR NEVER. "A NATION ONCE AGAIN"'

Churchill was always one to seize an opportunity. The Japanese attack on Pearl Harbor on 7 December 1941 is famous for bringing the Americans into the war. For Churchill that held the prospect of victory, and he later described how he went to bed that night 'and slept the sleep of the saved and thankful'.

However, before going to bed, he was clearly thinking about other ways of using this momentous news. The Free State of Ireland had come into existence in 1922, with Northern Ireland remaining part of the United Kingdom. With the outbreak of war, Ireland had opted for neutrality, maintaining diplomatic relations with Germany. To Churchill, this was infuriating. It meant the British Navy had no access to Irish ports, thereby making it much more difficult to defend shipping in the Atlantic against German U-boats, while Ireland could also potentially be used as a base for covert Nazi operations against Britain.

Here then was a chance to capitalize on strong Irish–American links. Perhaps President de Valera could be persuaded to join an alliance with the United States. If so, couching it in these terms and suggesting unity with Britain might not have been the wisest choice. The last thing that de Valera wanted was to become part of the United Kingdom. Then again, was Churchill hinting at the possibility of a united Ireland? It seems more likely, given that this message was sent at 12:20am, that he was simply swept up in the moment and articulating a vision of the two independent countries of the British Isles marching side by side. If so, he was to be disappointed. De Valera did not reply and Ireland remained neutral until the end of the war. Nevertheless, it remains a message that captures Churchill's sense of the moment and flair for the dramatic.

7: from Winston to Éamon de Valera, 8 December 1941 (CHAR 20/46/41)

TYPEX TELEGRAM
FROM: D.O.
TO: EIRE (REP.)
(~~Sent~~ 12.20 a.m. 8th ~~Dec.~~, 1941.)
MOST IMMEDIATE.
~~No. 120.~~
~~Following from~~ Prime Minister for Mr. De Valera Personal Private and Secret. Begins.

Now is your chance. Now or never. "A nation once again". Am very ready to meet you at any time. ~~Ends.~~

'BURN THIS LETTER WHEN YOU HAVE READ IT'

Pearl Harbor did mark the beginning of one of the closest political and military relationships in modern history. Churchill spent Christmas 1941 at the White House. He and the President kept late hours as they discussed the world's problems, much to the annoyance of the First Lady, Eleanor Roosevelt. When President Roosevelt inadvertently entered Churchill's room to find him emerging from his bath, Winston allegedly quipped that the Prime Minister of Great Britain had nothing to hide from the President of the United States.

Churchill certainly sought to share intelligence. On his return from Washington, he confirmed with 'C' that Britain was already sharing her cipher machines with the Americans. 'C' was Sir Stewart Menzies, the head of the British Intelligence Service and the inspiration for 'M' in the James Bond books and films. Churchill also wrote to Roosevelt discreetly warning him that the British had broken the American diplomatic codes. If Britain had managed to do this, then the Germans or Japanese might have done so too. It was a delicate matter, as Churchill was effectively admitting that the British had been spying on the United States, and he was at pains to tell the President that such activities had stopped as soon as the two countries had become allies.

This document illustrates the beginnings of a new relationship in intelligence sharing: one that persists to this day. Yet it was just one aspect of an alliance that would also see the establishment of a Combined Chiefs of Staff, joint planning and the appointment of theatre commanders with overall responsibility for both British and American forces. The two countries were now really mixed up together.

8: from Winston to President Roosevelt, 25 February 1942 (CHAR 20/52/17-19)

February 25, 1942

My dear Mr. President,

One night when we talked late, you spoke of the importance of our cipher people getting into close contact with yours. I shall be very ready to put any expert you care to nominate in touch with my technicians. Ciphers for our two Navies have been and are continually a matter for frank discussion between our two Services. But diplomatic and military ciphers are of equal importance and we appear to know nothing officially of your versions of these. Some time ago, however, our experts claimed to have discovered the system and constructed some tables used by your Diplomatic Corps. From the moment when we became allies, I gave instructions that this work should cease. However, danger of our enemies having achieved a measure of success cannot, I am advised, be dismissed.

I shall be grateful if you will handle this matter entirely yourself, and if possible burn this letter when you have read it. The whole subject is secret in a degree which affects the safety of both of our countries. The fewest possible should know.

I take advantage of the Ambassador's homeward journey to send you this by his hand, to be delivered into yours personally.

(Sgd.) Winston S. Churchill

'I DO NOT WANT THE LION AT THE MOMENT'

Prime Ministers receive a lot of gifts and Churchill was no exception. Among them were a cabinet of cigars from Cuba that had to be tested by scientists to make sure that they were not poisoned, a mouldy polar bear skin from Canada and a duck-billed platypus that died en route to Britain from Australia. One living gift to Churchill that survived was an African lion called Rota. The 10th Duke of Devonshire presented the animal in his capacity as a member of the Zoological Society of London, presumably in celebration of the recent Allied victories in North Africa.

In reality, this was a publicity stunt that benefited all parties (except Rota) and Churchill accepted on condition that the animal would be kept at London Zoo. His letter to the Duke is a great example of his wit and humour, dryly noting that he had no need of the lion at present at Downing Street or Chequers, due to the prevailing 'Ministerial calm', but noting that the zoo was not far away and that circumstances might arise in which he would have great need of it.

You can almost hear him dictating the letter, a cigar in one hand and perhaps a glass of whisky in the other. Churchill spent much of the war managing tensions between the big beasts in his Cabinet, men like the Conservative business leader Lord Beaverbrook or the Labour Trade Unionist Ernest Bevin, and there must have been moments when he felt like unleashing a lion.

On his eightieth birthday, in 1954, Churchill would claim that the British people had shown the lion's heart during the war, but that he had 'had the luck to be called upon to give the roar' and to suggest 'to the lion the right places to use his claws'. Rota was still alive. He died shortly afterwards, was stuffed and is now on display at the Lightner Museum in Florida.

9: from Winston to the Duke of Devonshire, 13 February 1943 (CHUR 1/58B/429)

13 Feb. 1943

Mr dear Eddie,

I shall have much pleasure in becoming the possessor of the lion, on the condition that I do not have to feed it or take care of it, and that the Zoo makes sure that it does not get loose.

You are quite right in your assumption that I do not want the lion at the moment either at Downing Street or at Chequers, owing to the Ministerial calm which prevails there. But the Zoo is not far away, and situations may arise in which I shall have great need of it.

I hope to come see the lion sometime when the weather is better, also my black swans.

I consider you personally bound to receive the lion at Chatsworth should all else fail.

Yours ever,

Winston

FEEDING ROTA THE LION, C. 1943.

'A MAN WHO HAS TO PLAY AN EFFECTIVE PART IN
TAKING, WITH THE HIGHEST RESPONSIBILITY, GRAVE
AND TERRIBLE DECISIONS OF WAR MAY NEED THE
REFRESHMENT OF ADVENTURE'

Churchill's lion heart was on display in June 1944. The Allies were
about to liberate France. D-Day was imminent and Churchill was
determined to accompany the invasion force himself. Plans were
made for the British Prime Minister to board HMS *Belfast* on D
minus 1, originally scheduled for 4 June, before transferring to
a destroyer for a short tour of the beaches. It was not popular.
The military commanders did not want the added burden and
responsibility of having Churchill anywhere near the action.

Churchill stuck to his guns. He realized that constitutionally
the only person who could stop him was the King and so he used
a Royal Audience on 30 May to try and enlist the support of his
Sovereign, suggesting that the two of them might go together.
Sir Alan Lascelles, the King's Private Secretary, quickly talked
George VI out of the idea. It then took two very personal and
handwritten appeals from the King, the second sent as late
as 2 June, before Churchill conceded. When he did, it was
with reservations and bad grace, grudgingly deferring to His
Majesty's 'wishes and indeed commands' while protesting that,
'I ought to be allowed to go where I consider it necessary to the
discharge of my duty'. Later, he reflected that: 'A man who has
to play an effective part in taking, with the highest responsibility,
grave and terrible decisions of war may need the refreshment of
adventure. He may need also the comfort that when sending
so many others to their death he may share in a small way their
risks.'

Churchill needed the release of action. He was finally able to
inspect the Normandy beachhead on 12 June. As a young Home
Secretary in January 1911, he had been criticized for personally
supervising a police siege of some anarchists in London. Now,

thirty-three years later and aged almost seventy, he still could not resist the smell of gunpowder.

10: from King George VI to Winston, 2 June 1944 (CHAR 20/136/4)

June 2nd 1944

My dear Winston,

I want to make one more appeal to you not to go to sea on D day. Please consider my own position. I am a younger man than you, I am a sailor, and as King I am the head of all three Services. There is nothing I would like better than to go to sea but I have agreed to stay at home; is it fair that you should then do exactly what I should have liked to do myself? You said yesterday afternoon that it would be a fine thing for the King to lead his troops into battle, as in old days; if the King cannot do this, it does not seem to me right that his Prime Minister should take his place.

Then there, is your own position. You will see very little, you will run a considerable risk, you will be inaccessible at a critical time when vital decisions might have to be taken, and however unobtrusive you may be, your mere presence on board is bound to be a very heavy additional responsibility to the Admiral and Captain.

As I said in my previous letter, your being there would add immeasurably to my anxieties, and your going without consulting your colleagues in the Cabinet would put them in a very difficult position which they would justifiably resent.

I ask you most earnestly to consider the whole question again, and not let your personal wishes, which I very well understand lead you to depart from your own high standard of duty to the State.

Believe me

Your very sincere friend

George R.I.[Rex Imperator]

BUCKINGHAM PALACE

June 2nd 1944

My dear Winston,

I want to make one more appeal to you not to go to sea on D day. Please consider my own position. I am a younger man than you, I am a sailor, & as King I am the head of all the Services. There is nothing I would like better than to go to sea but I have agreed to stay at home; is it fair that you should then do exactly what I should have liked to do myself?

You said yesterday afternoon that it would be a fine thing for the King to lead his troops into battle, as in old days; if the King cannot do this, it does not seem to me right that his Prime Minister should take his place.

Then there is your own position. You will see very little, you will run a considerable risk, you will be inaccessible at a critical time when vital decisions might have to be taken, & however unobtrusive you may be, your mere presence on board is bound to be a very heavy additional responsibility to the Admiral & Captain.

As I said in my previous letter, your being there would add immeasurably to my anxieties, & your going without consulting your colleagues in the Cabinet would put them in a very difficult position which they would justifiably resent.

I ask you most earnestly to consider the whole question again, & not let your personal wishes, which I very well understand, lead you to depart from your own high standard of duty to the State.

Believe me

Your very sincere friend

George R.I.

11: from Winston to King George VI, 3 June 1944 (CHAR 20/136/6-8)

3 June 1944

Sir,

I must excuse myself for not having answered Your Majesty's letter earlier. It caught me just as I was leaving by the train and I have been in constant movement ever since. I had a despatch rider standing by in order to take it to you tonight.

Sir, I cannot really feel that the first paragraph of your letter takes sufficient account of the fact that there is absolutely no comparison in the British Constitution between a Sovereign and a subject. If Your Majesty had gone, as you desire, on board one of your ships in this bombarding action, it would have required the Cabinet approval beforehand and I am very much inclined to think, as I told you, that the Cabinet would have advised most strongly against Your Majesty going.

On the other hand, as Prime Minister and Minister of the Defence, I ought to be allowed to go where I consider it necessary to the discharge of my duty, and I do not admit that the Cabinet have any right to put restrictions on my freedom of movement. I rely on my own judgment, invoked in many serious matters, as to what are the proper limits of risk which a person who discharges my duties is entitled to run. I must most earnestly ask Your Majesty that no principle shall be laid down which inhibits my freedom of movement when I judge it necessary to acquaint myself with conditions in the various theatres of war. Since Your Majesty does me the honour to be so much concerned about my personal safety on this occasion, I must defer to Your Majesty's wishes and indeed commands. It is a great comfort to me to know that they arise from Your Majesty's desire to continue me in your service. Though I regret that I cannot go, I am deeply grateful to Your Majesty for the motives which have guided Your Majesty in respect of

Your Majesty's humble and devoted Servant and Subject,

[n.s.]

CHURCHILL'S CABINET WITH KING GEORGE VI, 1944.

'EVER SINCE 1907, I HAVE IN GOOD TIMES AND BAD TIMES, BEEN A SINCERE FRIEND OF FRANCE'

It might have been expected that D-Day would bring the British and French closer together. It was, after all, the moment that both Churchill and Charles de Gaulle, the leader of the Free French, had been fighting for since the dark days of June 1940. France's surrender had led to her domination by Germany, with Paris occupied and the country reduced to a rump state ruled from Vichy. General de Gaulle, previously only a junior minister, had fled to Britain and raised the standard of resistance. Churchill had feted him as a man of destiny and given him shelter in London, but the two strongmen, each the living embodiment of their country's national honour, had clashed repeatedly.

De Gaulle's relationship with Roosevelt was even worse. The American President refused to recognize the general and his Free French Committee of National Liberation as the legitimate government of France. Things had come to a head just before D-Day. De Gaulle had only been told of the date and details at the last moment and arrived 'bristling' from his headquarters in Algiers. In an angry meeting, Churchill threatened to side with the Americans over the future of France and told him that 'each time we have to choose between Europe and the open sea, we shall always choose the open sea'. He urged de Gaulle to visit Washington and resolve issues with the President, while de Gaulle refused to cooperate with General Eisenhower in establishing civil authority in France.

Yet, for all the disagreement, Churchill and de Gaulle did have a mutual respect and admiration. In November 1944, they walked side by side down the Avenue des Champs-Élysées in Paris to celebrate its liberation. In spite of all his focus on the 'special relationship' with the United States, Churchill was always a Francophile. He loved French food and wine, and the atmosphere and climate of the South of France, while Napoleon remained his greatest hero. Nor did he always agree with the Americans.

12: from Winston to General Charles de Gaulle, 16 June 1944 (CHAR 20/137C/288)

16 June 1944

Dear General de Gaulle,

 ... I had high hopes when you arrived that we might have reached some basis of collaboration, and that I might have been of assistance to the French Committee of National Liberation in coming to more friendly terms with the Government of the United States. I am grieved that these hopes have not been realized except that there is a possibility that the discussion on an expert level may arrive at some modification of the present deadlock.

Ever since 1907, I have in good times and bad times, been a sincere friend of France, as my words and actions show, and it is to me an intense pain that barriers have been raised to an association which to me was very dear. Here in this visit of yours, which I personally arranged, I had the hope that there was a chance of putting things right. Now I have only the hope that it may not be the last chance.

If nevertheless I may presume to offer advice, it would be that you should carry out the visit which has been planned to

President Roosevelt and try to establish for France those good relations with the United States which are a most valuable part of her inheritance.

You may count on any assistance I can give in this matter, which is one of great consequence to the future of France.

Believe me,

Yours very sincerely,

SIGNED: WINSTON S. CHURCHILL

WITH GENERAL CHARLES DE GAULLE IN MARRAKESH, 1944.

'THUS TWO-THIRDS OF OUR FORCES ARE BEING MIS-EMPLOYED FOR AMERICAN CONVENIENCE, AND THE OTHER THIRD IS UNDER AMERICAN COMMAND'

Like Napoleon, Churchill enjoyed being close to the scene of the action. August 1944 found him visiting Italy and watching the Allied landings in the South of France. It was an operation he opposed. Churchill did not want more troops diverted to France. He wanted a continued advance up the spine of Italy. In part, this was because the armies in Italy were under British command, whereas the American General Eisenhower led those in France. Yet he also wanted to maintain a strategy of fighting on several fronts, knowing that this is what had defeated Napoleon.

As this full and frank letter to Clementine reveals, Churchill was becoming increasingly frustrated at his inability to influence grand strategy. Britain and her Empire had been at war for nearly five years, but the Allied effort was increasingly dominated by American and Soviet men and material, with the important decisions taken in Washington and Moscow.

Churchill's trip to the Italian sunshine had clearly done him good, but physically the stress and strain of war had taken a toll. He had almost died of pneumonia in North Africa at the end of 1943. Ultimately, what kept him going was his determination to deliver victory and his belief in his ability to influence his allies. He summed it up best himself in a quote recorded by his friend Violet Bonham Carter: 'There I sat with the great Russian bear on one side of me with paws outstretched, and, on the other side, the great American buffalo, and between the two sat the poor little English donkey, who was the only one, the only one of the three, who knew the right way home.'

13: from Winston to Clementine, 17 August 1944 (CSCT 2/33)

17 Aug. 1944   Italy [Naples]

PERSONAL

My darling,

We have had a busy but delightful time since we arrived here. A very comfortable guest-house, formerly the villa of a wealthy Fascist, now in a concentration camp, was got ready for us ... The few days we spent in Naples were relieved by a lovely expedition to the island of Ischia on the first day, and the second to Capri. I thought the Blue Grotto wonderful. We have had altogether four bathes which have done me all the good in the world. I feel greatly refreshed and am much less tired than when I left England.

On the 14th I flew with two of my party to Ajaccio [Corsica]. (Do you remember when we went to see Napoleon's house there in 1910?) ... I went out in a destroyer, taking with me two important Americans who arrived at the last minute and were at a loose end. The journey takes five hours, and a little after one o'clock we found ourselves in an immense concourse of ships all sprawled along 20 miles of coast with poor San Tropez in the centre.

... We traversed the whole front and saw the panorama of the beautiful shores with smoke rising from many fires started by the shelling and artificial smoke being loosed by the landing troops and the landing craft drawn up upon the shore. But we saw it all from a long way off. If I had known beforehand what the conditions would be I would have requested a picket-boat from the RAMILLIES, when I could have gone with perfect safety very much nearer to the actual beaches.

...

If you reflect upon what I have said at different times on strategic questions you will see that Eisenhower's operations have been a diversion for this landing instead of the other way round as the American Chiefs of staff imagined ... If I had had my way the armies now cast on shore 400 miles from Paris would have come in at St Nazaire in about a week and greatly widened the front of our advance with corresponding security against German movement east of Paris ...

...

What tremendous events are taking place in France! The Eike [Eisenhower]-Monty [sic] operations appear to be the greatest battle of the war and may result in the destruction of the German power in France. Such a victory will have effects in many directions, one of which undoubtedly will be more mutual respect between the Russians and the Anglo-American democracies.

... This visit of mine to the President is the most necessary one that I have ever made since the very beginning as it is there that various differences that exist between the Staffs, and also between me and the American Chiefs of Staff, must be brought to a decision. We have three armies in the field. The first is fighting under American Command in France, the second under General Alexander is relegated to a secondary and frustrated situation by the United States' insistence on this landing ~~of ten Divisions~~ on the Riviera. The third on the Burmese frontier is fighting in the most unhealthy country in the world under the worst possible conditions to guard the American ~~pipe~~ air line over the Himalayas into their very over-rated China. Thus two-thirds of our forces are being mis-employed for American convenience, and the other third is under American Command ... These are delicate and serious matters to be handled between friends in careful and patient personal discussion. I have no doubt we shall reach a good conclusion, but you will see that life is not very easy ...

...

I hope to remedy this. With tender love
Your ever loving husband
W

ON THE ITALIAN FRONTLINE, 1944.

'NO MORE LET US FALTER! FROM MALTA TO YALTA! LET NOBODY ALTER!'

The road to victory lay through Yalta in the Crimea, where Churchill, Roosevelt and Stalin met in February 1945 to discuss the final stages of the conflict and to decide the fate of the post-war world.

Churchill began the final year of the war with a lively rhyming exhortation to the President. He had arranged to meet Roosevelt in Malta before the conference because he wanted to coordinate their strategy ahead of discussions with the Russians.

In the event, these would be difficult meetings for Churchill. The British Prime Minister was increasingly concerned about the Soviet domination of Eastern Europe, and particularly Poland for which Britain had gone to war. Roosevelt's focus was on withdrawing American troops from Europe and winning Soviet help for the defeat of Japan in the Pacific. Churchill wanted to rebuild the British Empire and strengthen the Anglo-American relationship; Roosevelt was intent on bringing the Russians into the new United Nations organization. The two men remained friends but both were suffering from frail health. Roosevelt would die just four months later. Malta and Yalta would be their last meetings.

The war was now ending. Victory in Europe was in sight and would arrive in May 1945. However, new storm clouds were gathering. Yalta did not alter the realities on the ground. Privately, Churchill began to worry and warn about the prospects of a Soviet iron curtain descending across Europe or even of a third world war.

At home, he was facing criticism from Conservatives for failing to stop the Soviets in Poland and from Labour for using British forces to suppress a communist uprising in Greece. It was becoming difficult to hold his coalition government together.

14: telegram from Winston to President Roosevelt, 1 January 1945 (CHAR 20/210/6)

1 January 1945
AMENDED DISTRIBUTION
PRIME MINISTER TO PRESIDENT ROOSEVELT   No. 871
Personal and Top Secret   1.1.45

We shall be delighted if you will come to Malta. I shall be waiting on the quay. You will also see the inscription of your noble message to

Malta of a year ago. Everything can be arranged to your convenience. No more let us falter! From Malta to Yalta! Let nobody alter!

...

'YOU MAY BE SURE I SHALL ALWAYS ENDEAVOUR TO PROFIT BY YOUR COUNSELS'

In January 1945, Clement Attlee, the Deputy Prime Minister and Labour Party leader, sent a scathing letter to Churchill, criticizing his running of the Cabinet. It runs to six pages and systematically sets out Attlee's objections one after the other. Churchill was not reading his papers, he was rambling in the meetings and he was undermining collective government by acting on the advice of Conservative ministers outside of the War Cabinet.

Churchill's reply to this letter is a masterstroke. Rather than attempt an equally detailed response, he simply thanks Attlee and writes, '*You may be sure I shall always endeavour to profit by your counsels.*'

Yet, that is not the whole story. Churchill's Private Secretary, Jock Colville, was present when his boss received Attlee's letter and describes the incident in a document that survives in his papers. According to Colville, Churchill was furious at receiving Attlee's letter. Initially, he sat down to make a full reply – a point-by-point rebuttal, and such a draft survives. However, first Brendan Bracken, then Lord Beaverbrook, and finally Clementine all told Churchill that Attlee was right. Whereupon, Churchill fired off his single-line dismissal and turned to Colville with the words, 'Well I'm deserted by my friends and even by my wife ... let us think no more of either Attler or Hitlee, let us go off and see the movies.'

Colville's retelling, perhaps with embellishments, of this story is a testament to the way in which Churchill's character was able to win over those around him. His idiosyncrasies, his humour, his determination, his energy and his sheer bloody-mindedness shine through these contemporary accounts.

15: from Clement Attlee to Winston, 19 January 1945 (CHUR 2/4/86-89)

19 January 1945
Private and Personal

Mr dear Prime Minister

I have had it in mind for some time to write to you with regard to the present methods of dealing with matters requiring Cabinet decisions ...

I am stating the views I hold bluntly and frankly as I consider that it is my duty to do so. I am sure that you will not resent plain speaking.

My complaint relates mainly but not wholly to the method of dealing with civil affairs. I quite understand that, occupied so heavily as you are with the military conduct of the war and with relations with our Allies, you cannot give as much time as you wish to civil affairs. But that being so, I should have thought that you would have reposed some confidence in your Cabinet colleagues, but you seem to exhibit very scanty respect for their judgment ...

... At these committees we endeavour and, I claim, succeed in the vast majority of cases in reaching agreement and in subordinating Party views to the general interest. This applies to Ministers of all Parties in the Government. It is quite exceptional for Party issues to arise acutely. The conclusions of the Committees are brought to the Cabinet in memoranda which we all try to keep as concise as possible. What happens then?

Not infrequently there is delay, sometimes unnecessary delay before they reach the agenda. When they are reached it is exceptional for you to have read them and not infrequently you have not read even the note prepared for your information. The result is that much time is wasted in explaining what the paper is about. Sometimes a phrase catches your eye which evokes a disquisition only slightly connected with point at issue. The result is long delays and unnecessarily long Cabinets.

There is, however, a serious constitutional point here. In the eyes of the country and in fact the eight members of the War

Cabinet are responsible for decisions. I have assured Conservative members who approached me being disturbed at rumours of the influence of some non Cabinet Ministers, that this was so in fact, but, if the present practices continues, I shall be in a difficulty.

It is quite wrong that there should be a feeling among Ministers and Civil Servants that it is more important to gain the support [of] Ministers who are thought to have the ear of the Prime Minister than of members of the War Cabinet.

I have written very frankly to you on my own account, but I know that the views which I have expressed are not confined to myself. We are in a period when difficulties are increasing. I do not think that you can complain of any lack of loyalty on my part. I think your cabinet colleagues have the right to ask that in matters to which you cannot give personal attention, you should trust them.

Please excuse rough typing as I have written this myself for your eye alone.

Yours in all loyalty

Clement R. Attlee

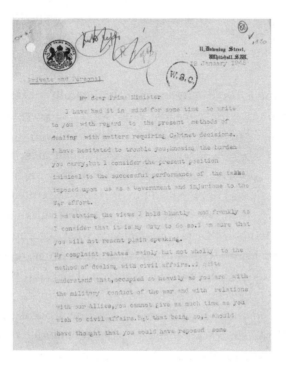

CHURCHILL'S WAR CABINET, 1941 WITH ATTLEE ON HIS LEFT.

16: from Winston to Attlee, 20 January 1945 (draft, not sent) (CHUR 2/4/82-85)

20 January 1945
First Edition
<u>PRIVATE</u>

My dear Lord President,

I thank you for your letter and for the advice it contains, which of course I will carefully consider. I thoroughly agree with you about the importance of frankness and even bluntness in time of war.

I am very ready to admit my own shortcomings in the matter of civil affairs. The great mass of war and foreign business, as well as ~~all~~ the other tasks which fall to me, including heavy Parliamentary work, have made it very difficult for me to follow the details of all the legislative and other proposals which your Committee bring to the Cabinet. I note what you say as to my laxity in these matters, and, heavy and exhausting as is my present burden, I will try my best to be better acquainted with these subjects in the future, so as not to take up your valuable time in explaining them to me in the Cabinet. *I need scarcely say I am deeply conscious of my own failings and that I will certainly try to live up to the standards you require.*

...

I know it is vexatious when one holds such very strong and clear opinions, as you and your colleagues do, and ~~are all~~ *when all are* united by one general theme of far-reaching political doctrine, to have criticisms of ~~a bold strong~~ an outspoken and controversial character advanced against you. Yet it seems to me that there is no reason why, in a *Coalition* Cabinet, both sides of Party opinion should not be expressed; and I could not accept the suggestion that once the Lord President's Committee had pronounced upon a subject, the Cabinet had no rights and the matter must be taken as settled.

In the result, you have very little to complain of, for *when* both these Ministers I have referred to have stated the Party case with their special view, as also do the Whips on occasion, ~~and~~ in nearly every case the decision has gone the way you wished. Therefore I hope that I may make an appeal to your patience and good nature during the *short* remaining time that our common task endures.

...

Once more thanking you for your advice and kind expressions, Believe me,

17: from Winston to Attlee, 22 January 1945 (ATLE 2 / 2 / 22)

January 22, 1945

My dear Lord President,

I have to thank you for your Private and Personal letter of January 19. You may be sure I shall always endeavour to profit by your counsels.

Yours sincerely,

(Sgd.) Winston S. Churchill

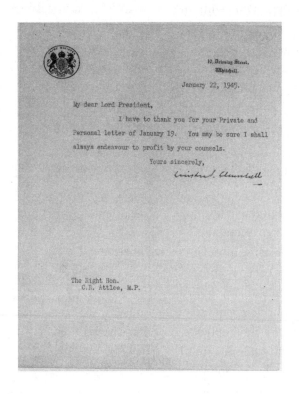

CHAPTER SEVEN

AFTERMATH AND LEGACY (1945–64)

'HERE IS THE ROCK OF SAFETY'

The 1945 General Election swept the Labour Party to power. The British people wanted peace and a government that would prioritize the building of a new society. Once again, Churchill had become yesterday's man. It was a cruel blow. Clementine Churchill suggested that, after five years of unrelenting pressure, it might be a blessing in disguise; Winston replied that it was certainly effectively disguised to him. He thought he had more to give and wanted to remain at the centre of events.

Clement Attlee became Prime Minister and Ernest Bevin, who had served in Churchill's coalition government as Minister for Labour, became Foreign Secretary. The two of them realized that Churchill remained one of the most famous men in the world and they made sure, despite their party-political differences, to consult him on matters of international affairs. In this letter to Bevin, Churchill outlines his vision for continuing and strengthening the Anglo-American alliance, seeing it as the most effective counterweight to the Russian threat. The new reality was that the United States was now far more powerful than the British Commonwealth, a huge change since the days of his youth, but this did not stop Churchill arguing for an equal partnership (including sharing military bases around the world).

This was the vision that he would share publicly just a few months later, on 5 March 1946, when he delivered his most famous post-war speech at Westminster College, Fulton, Missouri. It is now best known for its passage about a Soviet 'iron curtain' descending across the European continent, but the title of the address was actually 'The Sinews of Peace' and Churchill's main theme was that world security depended on the maintenance of the wartime special relationship between Britain and the United States.

1: from Winston to Ernest Bevin, 13 November 1945 (CHUR 2/2/41-44)

<u>Most Secret</u>
November 13, 1945

Dear Ernest,
    Thank you for sending me the telegrams, which I have duly burnt.

1   The long-term advantage to Britain and the
    Commonwealth is to have our affairs so interwoven
    with those of the United States in external and strategic
    matters, that any idea of war between the two countries
    is utterly impossible, and that in fact, however the matter
    may be worded, we stand or fall together. It does not seem
    likely that we should have to fall. In a world of measureless
    perils and anxieties, here is the rock of safety.

2   From this point of view, the more strategic points we
    hold in joint occupation, the better ... Although the
    United States is far more powerful than the British
    Commonwealth, we must always insist upon coming in
    on equal terms. We should press for Joint occupation at
    all points in question rather than accept the exclusive
    possession by the United States ...

3   I do not agree with the characteristic Halifax slant that
    we should melt it all down into a vague United Nations
    Trusteeship. This ignores the vital fact that a special and
    privileged relationship between Great Britain and the
    United States makes us both safe for ourselves and more
    influential as regards building up the safety of others
    through the international machine. The fact that the British
    Commonwealth and the United States were for strategic
    purposes one organism, would mean:-

a. that we should be able to achieve more friendly and trustful relations with soviet Russia, and

b. that we could build up the United Nations organization around us and above us with greater speed and success. "Whom God hath joined together, let no man put asunder". Our duties to mankind and all States and nations remain paramount, and we shall discharge them all the better hand in hand.

4 ... The future of the world depends upon the fraternal association of Great Britain and the Commonwealth with the United States. With that, there can be no war. Without it, there can be no peace ...

You are indeed fortunate that this sublime opportunity has fallen to you, and I trust the seizing of it will ever be associated with your name. In all necessary action you should count on me, if I can be of any use.

Yours v[er]y sincerely,
Winston S. Churchill

SPEAKING UNDER THE WATCHFUL EYE OF ABRAHAM LINCOLN AT THE ALBERT HALL, 1944.

'IT WILL BE A GREAT SHOCK TO THE BRITISH NATION TO
FIND THEMSELVES, ALL OF A SUDDEN, STRIPPED OF THEIR
EMPIRE'

Churchill said during the war that he 'had not become the King's
First Minister to preside over the liquidation of the British
Empire'. Perhaps then it really was a blessing for him that he was
no longer Prime Minister in 1946. The global scene had shifted
and the emergence of the United Nations organization and of new
international laws and rights began the slow end of Empire. Attlee's
government faced strong independence movements in India and
many of the British colonies, while post-war Britain lacked the
political, military or economic will or moral right to continue with
its occupation of so many foreign lands.

The draft shows Churchill wrestling with the new realities. He
acknowledges that he had committed to granting Dominion status
to India during the war, and is honest that he had only done so
because of the Japanese threat and the need to rally all Indians to
the defence of the sub-continent. His two handwritten annotations
recording the failure of this policy suggest how much he had felt
stung by the Congress Party's independence movement under
Gandhi's leadership. The letter shows that he was still thinking in
terms of a 'British mission' in India, reverting to the hard-line views
he had held in the 1930s, opposing independence and warning of
civil war. He was wrong to try to stop the former and too late to
prevent the latter.

The draft shows that he was also concerned about removing
British troops from Egypt and Palestine (though he cut these from
the final text). For Churchill, the big issue was really about Britain
losing her power and prestige on the world stage. He was now
swimming against the tide. India and Pakistan achieved independence
in 1947. The British withdrew from Palestine and Israel became
an independent state in 1948. We will return to events in Egypt,
but the Empire that Churchill had served in as a young soldier was
being liquidated.

2: from Winston to Clement Attlee, 1 May 1946 (draft) (CHUR 2/42/54-56)

May 1, 1946

As we have had some private, friendly talks, I think it right to put down on paper a few points where I feel difference would arise between us:-

1   About India. *First*, I consider myself committed up to the Cripps Mission in 1942, though you know what a grief this was to me. However the imminence of Japanese invasion of India and the hope, *which failed*, of rallying all forces possible to Indian national defence compelled me to take the line I did. ~~All this failed~~ But everything stood on the basis of an Agreement between the great forces composing Indian life. If that agreement is not forthcoming, I must resume my full freedom to point out the dangers and evils of the abandonment by Great Britain of her mission in India.

     Secondly, we had always contemplated that a constitution would be framed of Dominion status and only when that was definitely established should the latent right of a dominion to quit the Empire or Commonwealth become operative. If, at the present time, you reach immediately a solution of independence, I should not be able to support this. I may add that the dangers of civil war breaking out in India on our departure are at least as great as those which are held by the Anglo-American Commission on Palestine to make a continuance of British or Anglo-American Mandate necessary.

2   About Egypt. ~~I could not myself support the evacuation of British troops and Air forces from the country. I consider that even if we consent, as may be necessary, to withdraw from Cairo, we must hold the canal Zone with British troops, though these might be incorporated in an Anglo-Egyptian force specially charged with that duty.~~

~~I was very glad to hear that there is no intention to alter the con-Dominion condominium in the Sudan.~~

3 About Palestine. ~~I strongly favour putting all possible pressure upon the United States to share with us the responsibility and burden of bringing about a good solution on the lines now proposed by the Anglo-American Commission. If adequate American assistance is not forthcoming, we are plainly unable to either carry out our pledge to the Jews of building up a national Jewish home in Palestine, allowing immigration according to absorptive capacity, of if we feel ourselves unable to bear single-handed all the burdens cast upon us by the new Commission's report, we have an undoubted right to ask to be relieved of the Mandate, which we hold from the now defunct League of Nations. On the other hand, from a strategic point of view, it would be necessary to treat this matter in conjunction with the situation reached in Egypt about the Canal Zone.~~

I earnestly hope that we shall not find ourselves suddenly confronted with far-reaching and irrevocable decisions in these fields, for it will be a great shock to the British nation to find themselves, all of a sudden, stripped of ~~the whole of~~ their Empire and position in the East on the morrow of their victory in the War.

W.S.C.

'I REVIVED THE ANCIENT AND GLORIOUS CONCEPTION OF A UNITED EUROPE'

The end of Empire and the Soviet domination of Eastern Europe forced Churchill to think about Britain's security. Since writing an article in 1930, he had been a consistent advocate of a United Europe. He believed that closer European union would strip away barriers to trade and get rid of the nationalist tensions that had led to two hugely destructive world wars. Initially, he had seen Britain as standing outside of this process and acting as a guarantor of European stability, now he felt that Britain had to play an active role in making it happen (though he was perhaps deliberately unclear about the precise role that Britain would play within this union). Speaking in Zurich in September 1946, Churchill had called for reconciliation between France and Germany. Twenty months later, in April 1948, he was pushing for a conference to explore greater union at The Hague (which would take place a few weeks later in May).

Churchill used his role as an international figure to advance the cause of European union, but his vision of increasing cooperation between national states brought him into conflict with those, like the former French Prime Minister socialist Léon Blum, who favoured a more federal approach and who feared Churchill's domination of the issue. Blum's public statement that Churchill's 'stamp of approval brought with it the danger that the European federation would have a character too narrowly Churchillian' had clearly annoyed Churchill, who was already struggling to get Clement Attlee and the British Labour government to attend the Hague gathering.

Ultimately, Churchill supported practical moves that brought the Western European countries closer together (like the Marshall Plan for American financial aid to Europe and the creation of NATO, a mutual defence pact between Western European countries and the United States). His United Europe movement was about creating the atmosphere that made closer cooperation possible, while leaving the detail for others to develop.

3: from Winston to Léon Blum, 7 April 1948 (CHAQ 2 / 2 / 5)

7 April 1948

My dear Monsieur Blum,

I have read what you have written in LE POPULAIRE and I feel it my duty to apprise you and your friends of some facts about the Movement for United Europe of which you may not be aware. You say, "Mr. Churchill has a character too original and too powerful for him not to leave his mark on everything he touches …"

"The stamp of his approval brought with it the danger that European federation would have a character too narrowly Churchillian. Thus is explained the embarrassment, circumspection and hesitation of the Labour Party and in consequence of international Socialism. The Federalist movement would have great difficulty in emerging from the shadow of a too illustrious name."

When at Zurich in September 1946 I revived the ancient and glorious conception of a United Europe ... I had no idea it would become a Party question. I thought it would become a movement and an inspiration on a level far above Party politics in any country. Indeed if we cannot rise above Party difference in a common cause on which we all agreed, how can we hope to bridge the fearful gulfs of reciprocal injuries between nations great and small, and then repair the ruin of Europe? ... It would be a disaster to a supreme and vital cause if ordinary, Party politics in Britain were to obstruct this great international movement.

Nothing could be more wrong and foolish than for the Socialist Parties of Europe to try to create and maintain a monopoly of a cause and policy which belongs not to local Parties, but to whole states and nations. The Socialist parties are not in a majority in any European country and they have no excuse to try to warn off and drive away all the other Parties of the Left, the Centre and the Right, without whose aid the results at which we all aim could not be achieved. To do this would be to imitate the Communist technique and the one-Party System. The idea that Europe could be united on a one-Party Socialist basis, fighting the Communists on the one hand and all the other Parties on the other, is of course absurd. You will need all the help you can get and we shall need all the comradeship of which we are worthy, if we are to win this great prize for all the peoples, for all the Parties "for all the men in all the lands."

For these reasons the Conservative Party in Britain have given their full support to Mr. Bevin in the policy of a Western European Union, which he has adopted. No-one is seeking to deprive him or the British Socialist Government of any credit which is theirs. The position of a Minister, holding the high executive Office of

Foreign Secretary, is quite different from that of a private person, even if he has the misfortune to be, to quote your flattering words, "too illustrious." The Minister has executive responsibility and has to act as well as speak. There will be great credit for Mr. Bevin, and indeed for all, if a good result is gained and Europe stands aloft once more in splendour. Those will be unworthy of the occasion and fall below the level of events, who allow Party feelings or personal likes and dislikes to stand in the way of the main result.

When we decided many months ago to attempt a Conference at the Hague, it was the best step open to private people to further the cause that has now been espoused by sixteen Governments and would be joined by many more if they were free. The British All-Party Committee, Conservatives, Liberals and Socialists alike, have always had the aim of keeping the whole movement above Party politics in England or in any other country. At the present time I understand that an important delegation of British Socialists will be present at the Hague in May. I do not believe that any particularist or sectarian differences will prevent a memorable demonstration in favour of the general purpose which we all share ...

I cannot feel that my own initiative has been harmful. You must remember that Mr. Marshall at his News conference on June 12, 1947 disclosed that my advocacy of the United States of Europe had influenced his development of the idea that Europeans should work out their own economic recovery and that the United States should extend financial help.

I feel greatly honoured to have been a link in setting in train the Marshall Plan upon which all our Governments are united and all our hopes depend.

The British Socialist Party have not threatened with disciplinary measures or victimization any of their members who may come to the Hague as individuals, and I trust that the French Socialist Party will allow full freedom to its own members; for I am sure that all who fall out of the line in these grave and melancholy times will expose themselves to the reproach of history ...

'INTERVENTION BY A GREAT STATE IN THE INTERNAL AFFAIRS OF A SMALL ONE IS ALWAYS QUESTIONABLE'

Attlee, Bevin and Blum were not the only major political figures corresponding with Churchill during the late 1940s. He also exchanged letters with President Truman. In December 1944, Churchill had spent his Christmas trying to negotiate a peace in Athens between the Greek nationalists and their communist rivals. His sympathies had lain with the nationalists and the British and Americans continued to support them as civil war persisted in the country, especially after the beginning of the Cold War between the West and Russia. In his letter, Churchill sets out his belief that large states must think very carefully before interfering in smaller states and that, if the Americans further intervene in Greece, they must do so with 'overwhelming power' as 'Not to do this is only to prolong the agony at immense expense'. He never believed in doing anything half-heartedly but it seems a prescient warning about the dangers of being dragged piecemeal into long conflicts – a problem that has since dogged Western leaders in countries like Vietnam and Afghanistan. In this instance, further American intervention in Greece did not prove necessary.

However, Churchill's use of overwhelming power extended to the atomic bomb. He felt that the Americans should use the advantage it gave them to exert pressure on the Russians. His view was that if Stalin believed that Truman was serious about using the weapon, he would not act against the West and this would 'ward off the catastrophe of a third world war'. In his reply to Churchill, Truman expressed himself as less pessimistic than Churchill about the possibility of a third world war as the Russians would not want 'to face complete destruction'.

Unfortunately, for both Churchill and Truman, the Russians successfully tested their own atomic bomb just two months later. Any window of American advantage had closed. Once again, the stakes had changed.

4: from Winston to President Truman, 29 June 1949 (CHUR 2/158/17-19)

29 June 1949

My dear Harry,

I feel I ought to send you the enclosed memorandum which has been written by a very able young member of our Party in the House of Commons, Mr. Alec Spearman, as the result of his visit to Greece. I should be grateful to you if you could, among your many preoccupations, find time to read it. I cannot vouch personally for the facts, but you have no doubt full information. In view of the very great possibility I undertook in 1944–45 to save Athens from falling a prey to the Communists, as it would have done, and in view of the adoption of this policy at great expense by the United States, I venture upon the following comment:-

Intervention by a great state in the internal affairs of a small one is always questionable and entails much complicated argument. If the great state thinks it right to intervene surely they should make their intervention effective by using the overwhelming power they have at their disposal. Not to do this is only to prolong the agony at immense expense and possibly to final disastrous conclusion. I hope you will consider this as it affects the future in many ways.

I was deeply impressed by your statement about not fearing to use the atomic bomb if need arose. I am sure this will do more than anything else to ward off the catastrophe of a third world war. I have felt it right to speak, as you have seen, in terms of reassurance for the immediate future, but of course I remain under the impression of the fearful dangers which impend upon us. Complete unity, superior force and the undoubted readiness to use it, give us the only hopes of escape. Without you nothing can be done.

Yours very sincerely,

Signed: Winston S. Churchill

WITH PRESIDENT HARRY TRUMAN.

5: from President Truman to Winston, 2 July 1949 (CHUR 2 / 158 / 22)

2 July 1949

Dear Winston,

I appreciated your good letter of the 29th most highly, and read the enclosed note on a visit to Greece by Mr. Alec Spearman with a great deal of interest.

I am in agreement with you that Greece must be kept from the hands of the Communists, and we expect to do everything possible to fulfill that objective.

I am not so pessimistic as you are about the prospects for a third world war. I rather think that eventually we are going to forget that idea, and get a realworld [sic] peace. I don't believe even the Russians can stand it to face complete destruction, which certainly would happen to them in the event of another war.

I hope you are in good health and that everything is going well with you. It is always a pleasure to hear from you.

Sincerely Yours,

Signed: Harry Truman

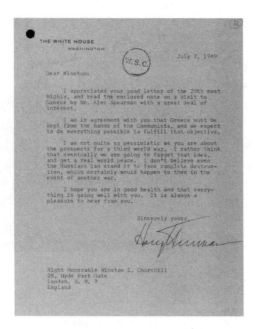

'FOR WHOEVER WINS THERE WILL BE NOTHING BUT BITTERNESS AND STRIFE'

Churchill certainly did not think of himself as finished. He was seventy-five years old in January 1950 but remained determined to return to No. 10 Downing Street as an elected peacetime Prime Minister. Clement Attlee had just called an election, after four and a half years of Labour Party government, and Churchill once again threw himself into campaigning, returning early from his holiday in Madeira to enter the political fray. Those in his inner circle were expected to join the fight. His son Randolph would lose to Michael Foot in Plymouth, while his son-in-law Christopher Soames would recover from his ulcer and win in Bedford.

Labour had introduced the National Health Service, reformed education and nationalized essential industries, but the domestic scene in Britain was one of continuing austerity with wartime reconstruction, housing shortages and rationing. The rise of communist China and escalating tensions in Korea and Vietnam dominated the international news. Churchill was clearly struggling to find the right message to send to the electorate 'for whoever wins there will be nothing but bitterness and strife, like men fighting savagely on a small raft which is breaking up'.

In the event, Labour won the February 1950 General Election but with a majority of just five. Churchill would have to wait until October 1951 for his election as Prime Minister. He committed to a policy of 'houses, red meat and not being scuppered'. With his own health starting to fail, and his famous levels of energy waning, he left the running of the economy largely to others and concentrated his efforts on international affairs. He wanted a renewal of the Anglo-American relationship and a 'parley at the summit' with the Russians.

6: from Winston to Clementine, 19 January 1950 (CSCT 2/38)

19 Jan 1950

My Darling,

Welcome home! And what a test of toil and trouble awaits you! I have not thought of anything in the week since I returned except politics, particularly the Tory Manifesto on which we have had prolonged discussions. One day we were nine hours in the dining room of No. 28 [Hyde Park Gate].

The Socialists are forcing the Election on to the most materialist lines. All bold treatment of topics in the public interest is very dangerous. The Liberals are running over four hundred candidates, of which at the outside seven will be elected, apart from the sixty who are working with us.

The Gallup Polls I showed you on the diagram have taken a big dip. Instead of being nine points ahead we are only three. This I think is due to Christmas and the fact that none of the evils of devaluation have really manifested themselves yet and are only on the way. How many seats the Liberal "splits" will cause us cannot be measured. All is in the unknown. However there would be no fun in life if we knew the end in the beginning.

... My Liberal opponent has withdrawn and gone to fight Herbert Morrison at Lewisham. He must be a very pugnacious fellow. We have a new one but I do not recall his name.

I have an immense programme but not more than I can carry. The broadcast speech is finished. I am planning to open my speaking campaign in the constituency with an address to the same lot of Headquarters staff and workers that we met the other night. This will enable me to make a nationwide speech on Saturday, January 28.

You will like to see Randolph's admirable opening speech. They now say that Foot is going to bolt to a safer seat. Randolph is coming for the weekend. June is staying in the constituency to electioneer with Arabella.

I was grieved to learn this morning from Christopher that he has a duodenal ulcer. Until he is photographed next week we cannot tell how serious it is. The doctor hopes that he will be able to fight. If not, Mary will have to fill the gap.

... I am much depressed about the country because for whoever wins there will be nothing but bitterness and strife, like men fighting savagely on a small raft which is breaking up. "May God save you all" is my prayer.

Come home & kiss me
Your ever loving
W

WEARING HIS SIREN SUIT AT HIS HOME CHARTWELL, KENT, 1950.

'I AM WRITING TO ASK IF YOU COULD CONSIDER GIVING
ME YOUR KIND SERVICES SO THAT I MAY HAVE SOME
PUPPIES BY YOU'

By the beginning of 1955, Churchill was clinging to political
office. His health had suffered another major setback following
a severe stroke in 1953. The Cabinet was pressing for a date
for his retirement and Anthony Eden was keen to become the
next Prime Minister. Churchill had not been able to persuade
President Eisenhower to back his proposal for a meeting with the
Soviet leadership and he was becoming increasingly alarmed by
the threat posed by the huge destructive power of the hydrogen
bomb.

Yet, when he grew weary of the world of men, he could
take comfort in his own animal kingdom. At Chartwell, there
were fish, black swans and pigs to feed. He owned racehorses,
calling one Pol Roger after his favourite champagne, and was
rarely without a budgerigar, a cat or a dog at his side. These
animals often shared his independent spirit. His budgerigar
Toby was famous for pecking and pooping on important visitors.
His miniature poodles Rufus I and later II (presumably named
for their Churchillian red hair) used to travel with him in the
back of his official car, disconcerting the secretaries with their
bad breath.

Churchill took a keen interest in the welfare of his animals,
and his hand can be sensed in this correspondence arranging a
romantic assignation between Rufus II and his would-be lover,
the poodle Jennifer of Post Green. Few dogs can have conducted
their courtships on Downing Street paper. In the end, the
relationship was not consummated. Jennifer as a standard rather
than miniature poodle was not felt to be a suitable pedigree for
Rufus. He was after all the pet of a Knight of the Garter and the
grandson of a Duke.

7: from Rufus of Chartwell to Jennifer of Post Green, March 1955 (CHUR 1/59/143-145)

VERY PRIVATE
March, 1955

My dear Jennifer,

On the 10th of April I shall be going to stay with a great friend of mine, Miss Lobban, who has very nice kennels in London. I should be very glad to receive you there, and Miss Lobban says she will make every arrangement for your comfort.

I am sorry I have not been able to write before, but my plans have been somewhat uncertain.

Looking forward to seeing you,

Yours very sincerely,

[n.s.]

TRAVELLING IN STYLE WITH HIS BELOVED POODLE, RUFUS II.

'TO RESIGN IS NOT TO RETIRE'

Churchill finally bowed to the inevitable and resigned. He hosted the young Queen Elizabeth and Prince Philip to a dinner at Downing Street and then, on 5 April 1955, chaired his final Cabinet meeting. Eden led the tributes on behalf of the assembled ministers saying that 'They would remember him always – for his magnanimity, for his courage at all times and for his unfailing humour, founded in his unrivalled mastery of the English language.' For his part, Churchill urged his colleagues to weave 'still more closely the threads which bound together the countries of the Commonwealth or, as he still preferred to call it, the Empire'. He also apparently declared, though it is not recorded in the official minutes, that 'Man is spirit' and advised his colleagues never to be separated from the Americans.

It is not surprising then that one of the last letters he drafted as Prime Minister, even if it was not sent, was this one to President Eisenhower. In it, he pledges to continue working for greater Anglo-American unity and against communism. These were aims that he saw as being identical and that informed his last great multi-volume work. Churchill's *History of the English-Speaking Peoples*, begun in the 1930s but finally published between 1956 and 1958, ends with a call for Anglo-American union, prefaced with the line 'the future is unknowable, but the past should give us hope'. As with nearly all his books, he was attempting to harness the past in order to influence the present and shape the future.

8: from Winston to President Eisenhower, April 1955 (draft) (CHUR 2/217/37-38)

April 1955

My dear Friend,

I have to thank you for your two memorable letters of March 22 and 29. By the time you get this very inadequate reply I shall have resigned my Office as Prime Minister and relinquished my direction of British policy. Anthony Eden and I have long been friends and lately even related by marriage; but quite apart from personal ties I feel it is my duty, as Leader of the Conservative Party, to make sure that my successor has a fair chance of leading the Conservatives to victory at the next Election, which, under the Quinquennial

Acts, falls at the end of October 1956 ... It will in many ways be a disaster to most of the causes with which we are both concerned if the Socialist Party in its present feebleness and disarray should again obtain what might be a long lease of power in Britain. I do not feel sure that our national vitality and wisdom would survive the event and the impression it would make on the world. At any rate I did not feel that I ought to overhang the situation unless I were prepared to lead the Party in the Election myself. This at my age I could not undertake to do. Hence I have felt it my duty to resign.

To resign is not to retire, and I am by no means sure that other opportunities may not come upon me to serve and influence those causes for which we have both of us worked so long. Of these the first is Anglo-American brotherhood, and the second is the arrest of the Communist menace. They are, I believe, identical.

'IT WILL BE AN ACT OF FOLLY, ON WHICH OUR WHOLE CIVILISATION MAY FOUNDER'

Anthony Eden does not seem to have heard Churchill's final words of advice. In November 1956, Anglo-French-Israeli forces attempted to seize control of the Suez Canal in Egypt (in response to the vital waterway having been nationalized by the Egyptian leader, Nasser). They did so without consulting the Americans and thereby invoked the wrath of Eisenhower. Overwhelming political and economic pressure from the United States resulted in a humiliating retreat that ultimately destroyed Eden's health and his premiership.

It is not clear to what extent Churchill supported military action against Nasser – his instincts are likely to have been in favour of it – but we do know that he is unlikely to have acted without the Americans and that he was horrified by the damage done to his 'special relationship'. His letter to Eisenhower, drafted with the help of his team, would have been encouraged by the British government and must count as one of his last official assignments. He followed it up with one last visit to the American President and the White House in 1959.

The changes Churchill had witnessed in his long life were immense. The world was now a smaller and more interconnected place. Missiles fired from Russia could destroy the West and vice versa. The British Empire was disappearing. The new superpowers of the United States and the Soviet Union were ascendant. There were times when this clearly depressed him and when he questioned whether he had achieved anything, but he still kept the black dog at bay by focusing on a more optimistic future.

9: from Winston to President Eisenhower, 22 November 1956 (draft)
(CHUR 2 / 217 / 141-142)

DRAFT
22 November 1956

My dear Ike

There is not much left for me to do in this world and I have neither the wish nor the strength to involve myself in the present political stress and turmoil. But I do believe, with unfaltering conviction, that the theme of the Anglo-American alliance is more important today than at any time since the war. You and I had some part in raising it to the plane on which it ~~until recently~~ has stood. Now, whatever the arguments adduced here and in the United States for or against Anthony's action in Egypt, it will be an act of folly, on which our whole civilisation may founder, to let events in the Middle East *become a gulf* between us ...

There seems to be growing misunderstanding and frustration on both sides of the Atlantic. If they be allowed to develop, the skies will darken indeed and it is the Soviet Union that will ride the storm. We should leave it to the historians to argue the rights and wrongs of all that has happened during the past years. What we must face is that at present these events have left a situation in the Middle East in which spite, envy and malice prevail on the one hand and our friends are beset by bewilderment and uncertainty for the future. The Soviet Union is attempting to move into this dangerous vacuum, for you must have no doubt that a triumph for Nasser is an even greater triumph for them.

The very survival of all we believe [in] may depend on our setting our minds to forestalling them. If we do not take immediate action in harmony, it is no exaggeration to say that we must expect to see the Middle East and the North African coastline under Soviet control and Western Europe placed at the mercy of the Russians. If at this juncture we fail in our responsibility to act positively and fearlessly we shall no longer be worthy of the leadership with which we are entrusted.

I write this letter because I know where your heart lies. You are now the only one who can so influence events both in UNO [United Nations Organisation] and the free world as to ensure that the great essentials are not lost in bickerings and pettiness among the nations. Yours is indeed a heavy responsibility and there is no greater believer in your capacity to bear it or *truer* well-wisher in your task than your old friend Winston S. Churchill.

W.S.C.

V-FOR-VICTORY WITH PRESIDENT DWIGHT EISENHOWER.

'EVEN A JOKE IN MY POOR TASTE CAN BE ENJOYED'
The idea for Churchill College in Cambridge was part of that
vision for the future. It was born of the fear that Britain was
lagging behind in science and technology, but also from the need
to find new interests for Winston Churchill and appropriate
ways to commemorate him. The idea was for a memorial to Sir
Winston Churchill, but a living memorial that he would help
create by chairing the Trustees and lending his name to the appeal
for funding.

The new foundation was embroiled in two controversies. Should it
admit women alongside men and so become the first co-educational
Cambridge college? There is evidence that Churchill, influenced by
Clementine, might have supported this, but Jock Colville wrote
to his fellow trustees that Cambridge had already swallowed two
revolutionary proposals in accepting a bias towards science and
engineering, and a high proportion of postgraduate students. To add
women to this mix would have the effect of dropping a '*hydrogen
bomb*' on the University. The issue was dropped and Churchill
became the last all-male college to be founded in Cambridge (though
subsequently the first all-male college in Cambridge to vote to admit
women, which it did in 1969, the first female students arriving
in 1972).

Then there was religion. This was the early 1960s. Churchill
was to be a forward-thinking and dynamic scientific community.
Should it have the traditional college chapel? The original
Trustees decided not, but the founding Fellows felt otherwise
and subsequently gave land to a legally separate Chapel Trust.
The issue did not go uncontested. Francis Crick, the famous
molecular biologist and – along with Watson – the man who
unravelled the structure of DNA, resigned his fellowship. He
took the point further by sending Churchill a letter joking that
the College would be better served by having a brothel for the
young men's physical needs, and enclosed the first donation to
the brothel (Hetairae) fund.

10: from Francis Crick to Winston, 12 October 1961 (CHUR 2/571/229-230)

Cambridge
12th October, 1961.

Dear Sir Winston,

It was kind of you to write. I am sorry you do not understand why I resigned.

To make my position a little clearer I enclose a cheque for ten guineas to open the Churchill College Hetairae fund. My hope is that eventually it will be possible to build permanent accommodation within the College, to house a carefully chosen selection of young ladies in the charge of a suitable Madam who, once the institution has become traditional, will doubtless be provided, without offence, with dining rights at the high table.

Such a building will, I feel confident, be an amenity which many who live in the college will enjoy very much, and yet the instruction need not be compulsory and none need enter it unless they wish. Moreover it would be open (conscience permitting) not merely to members of the Church of England, but also to Catholics, Non-Conformists, Jews, Moslems, Hindus, Zen Buddhists and even to atheists and agnostics such as myself.

And yet I cannot help feeling that when you pass on my offer to the other Trustees – as I hope you will – they may not share my enthusiasms for such a truly educational project. They may feel, being men of the world that to house such an establishment, however great the need and however correctly conducted, within the actual College would not command universal respect. They may even feel my offer of ten guineas to be a joke in rather poor taste.

But that is exactly my view of the proposal of the Trustees to build a chapel, after the middle of the 20th century, in a new College and in particular in one with a special emphasis on science. Naturally some members of the College will be Christian, at least for the next decade or so, but I do not see why the College should tacitly endorse their beliefs by providing them with special facilities. The churches in the town, it has been said, are half empty. Let them go there. It will be no further than they have to go to their lectures.

Even a joke in my poor taste can be enjoyed, but I regret that my enjoyment of it has entailed my resignation from the College which bears your illustrious name.

Understandably I shall not be present on Saturday. I hope it all goes well.

Yours Sincerely,

Francis Crick

'I SHALL PERSEVERE'

Winston was now retreating from such worldly problems. He sought the sunshine in the South of France, staying in luxury at the Hôtel de Paris in Monte Carlo or in the villas of old friends like Lord Beaverbrook. Too old to write or paint, he was looked after by his private secretary Anthony Montague Browne and by other members of what today might be called 'Team Churchill'. He had been befriended by the Greek shipping magnate Aristotle Onassis, who liked to collect famous names and sail them round the world in his yacht the *Christina*. Churchill wrote this letter just three days before setting off on his eighth and final cruise with Onassis around the Greek islands.

Clementine preferred not to accompany him on these trips. She was more puritan in her tastes. Winston clearly missed her. They had been married for almost fifty-five years and had been through an enormous amount together. The 18th June was the twenty-third anniversary of Churchill's 'Finest Hour' speech, in which he had rallied the British nation after the sudden fall of France in the summer of 1940. Now, as he entered the final stage of his long life, he had to show a different form of courage and perseverance. Separately, he described himself as being 'like an aeroplane at the end of its flight, in the dusk, with the petrol running out, in search of a safe landing'. This was his 'long sunset'.

11: from Winston to Clementine, 18 June 1963 (CSCT 2/50)

                                                      Hôtel de Paris
18 June 1963   Monte Carlo

Darling Clemmie

Thank you so much for your letter, which I received today. I do hope you are having a good rest and that the weather is better.

Here we have had on the whole sunny days, and I go for a daily drive with Anthony [Montague Browne]. We also sat in Max's garden [at La Capponcina] one afternoon, and the white cat sat with us.

Jock and Meg [Colville] and Nonie [Montague Browne] join us tomorrow, and I think we sail on Thursday night or Friday.

It has certainly been very pleasant and amusing using these very comfortable and princely rooms. I do wish that you had been filling the odd room.

We really must try ~~and~~ & get something [undecipherable deleted word] [?]fixed in a reasonable fashion. These places are so suited I do hope you will come in the long run.

— I shall [undecipherable deleted word] persevere.

With all my love – many kisses X X X X X

Your devoted

W

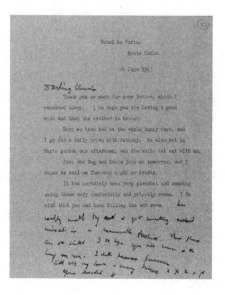

April 1955

WITH CLEMENTINE ON HIS LAST NIGHT AS PRIME MINISTER, 1955.

'I OWE YOU WHAT EVERY ENGLISHMAN, WOMAN & CHILD DOES – LIBERTY ITSELF'

At the end of his life, Churchill was surrounded by his family. He died peacefully at his London house in Hyde Park Gate on 24 January 1965 at the grand old age of ninety, seventy years to the day from the death of his father, Lord Randolph Churchill.

Churchill received a full State funeral and was buried alongside his parents in the small parish cemetery of Bladon in Oxfordshire. The graveyard is within sight of his birthplace at Blenheim Palace and the gardens where he had proposed to Clementine. His life had come full circle.

It seems fitting to end with this personal letter from his daughter Mary. It is the letter that Sir Martin Gilbert chose to quote at the conclusion of the eight-volume official biography. The aim of this selection has been to give some sense of the man behind the cigars and the famous speeches. In this moving letter, Mary seeks to reconcile her private love for her father with her admiration for him as a public figure. He would have liked her description of him as an Englishman, though to Churchill, England, Britain and the British Empire were often interchangeable, and he would have appreciated her stirring words and their implication that he had done something with his life and made history.

How would he have responded? Perhaps with his observation that 'The journey has been enjoyable and well worth making – once.'

12: from Mary Soames to her father, Winston, 8 June 1964 (CHUR 1 / 136 / 234-235)

June 8ᵗʰ 1964

My Darling Papa,

While I was in Russia a wonderful, unexpected cheque arrived from you. Thank you so very, very much for this marvellous and most welcome present – the fruit of your thoughts and labours. I am so moved that in addition to all you do, and have done for me, you should have given me this generous gift.

Darling Papa – you have indeed showered us with love, and make such wonderfully sound and far-seeing arrangements for your children and your children's children. I hope you have some satisfaction and contentment from all this; it is truly a 'house' whose strong walls have been built – every brick – by your genius and unceasing toil.

I have such a happy, full life – and we all love this home here – where the children can grow up in the liberty that only a country life can give – a place where Christopher can re-charge his batteries, and where we can both enjoy each other and our sweet children – And we know how great a part of this comfort and security we owe to you – and we bless and thank you for it.

I wish I could express more adequately my love and gratitude – but please believe me, they are real and deep; and in addition is all the feelings a daughter has for a loving, generous father, I owe you what every Englishman, woman & child does – liberty itself.

With love and gratitude from your

<u>Mary</u>

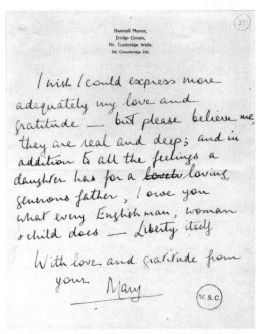

AT HOME WITH HIS FAMILY.

ABOUT THE EDITORS

JAMES DRAKE

James Drake is Founder of the Future Science Group, the Drake Foundation, the Drake Calleja Trust and Of Lost Time Ltd.

Some years ago, James acquired the letter archive of the former great tenor Enrico Caruso. His first instinct was to show it to the greatest contemporary lyric tenor, Joseph Calleja; James was inspired by his deep emotion at seeing the manuscripts. This crystallized his passion for connecting to the past through the power of personal historical correspondence and led him to establish Of Lost Time Ltd, a name inspired by his experience of handling an original draft for a portion of Proust's great novel, *In Search of Lost Time*. *Letters for the Ages: The Private and Personal Letters of Sir Winston Churchill* is the result of this journey, marrying James's fascination for the intimacy of personal correspondence with the life and wisdom of Winston Churchill.

To learn more visit:

James's website at www.JamesDrake.com

Drake Foundation – www.drakefoundation.org

Of Lost Time Ltd – www.oflosttime.com

Drake Calleja Trust – www.drakecallejatrust.org

ALLEN PACKWOOD

Allen Packwood BA, MPhil (Cantab), is a Fellow of Churchill College at the University of Cambridge, the Director of the Churchill Archives Centre, and a Fellow of the Royal Historical Society. He was awarded an OBE for services to archives and scholarship in the 2016 Queen's Birthday Honours. His book, *How Churchill Waged War*, was published by Pen & Sword in 2018.

INDEX

abdication crisis   156–7
Abyssinia (Ethiopia)   148
Allahabad Pioneer   51, 52
Amery, Leo   15
Anglo-Saxon Review, The   21
Asquith, Herbert   80, 100, 103, 115, 116, 117, 119, 124–5
letters to   100–2
atomic bomb   212, 213, 218
Attlee, Clement   197, 203, 215
letters from   198–9
letters to   200–2, 207–8

Baldwin, Stanley   137, 148–9, 151, 153, 156
letters to   157–8
Balfour, Arthur   108
Baring, Hugo   43, 45, 143
letters to   143–5
Barnes, Reginald   36, 45
Barnum's circus   12
Barrymore, Ethel   80
Beaverbrook, Lord (Max Aitken)   184, 197, 226
Bevin, Ernest   184, 203, 210, 211
letters to   204–5
Blenheim Palace   1, 84, 228
Blood, Bindon   51, 52
Blum, Léon   154, 155, 209
letters to   209–11
Boer War   67–8, 70–2
Spion Kop   70, 72
Bonar Law, Andrew   118, 125, 126, 134–5

Bonham Carter, Violet   193
Bracken, Brendan   197
British Empire   40, 135, 196, 206, 222
British Gazette   140
British Restaurants (Community Feeding Centres)   164
Brunswick Road school, Brighton   4, 6, 7
Buffalo Bill (William F. Cody)   10

Campbell-Bannerman, Henry   80
Carson, Edward   120
Cecil, Hugh   77
letter to   79
Chamberlain, Joseph   77–8
Chamberlain, Neville   155, 161, 163, 169
letters to   164–5, 170, 177–8
Chant, Laura Ormiston   56
Chartwell   4, 42, 136–7
animals   218
Chartwell Bulletins   146–8
China   151, 153, 215
Churchill, Clementine (née Hozier)   81, 84–5, 89, 91, 107, 157, 159, 197, 203, 226
letters from   120–4, 173–4
letters to   82, 83–4, 85–6, 90–1, 92–3, 95–8, 109–10, 112–15, 116–18, 128–30, 137–9, 146–7, 149–50, 152–3, 193–5, 216–17, 227
Churchill, Diana   84, 85, 90
Churchill, Gwendeline (Goonie)   109, 113

Churchill, Jack   1, 5, 6, 13, 16, 29, 30,
    40, 45, 71, 72, 132
  letters to   37–8
  in South Africa   70
Churchill, Marigold   131
Churchill, Randolph   xvii, 85, 90, 110,
    146, 147, 151, 152, 159, 215,
    217
  letters to   159–60
Churchill, Lady Randolph (Jennie
    Jerome, later Mrs George
    Cornwallis-West)   1, 6, 23, 44–5,
    75
  death of   131, 132
  financial issues   60, 61–2
  letters from   15–16, 24, 46, 76
  letters to   2–3, 7, 11–12, 13–14, 17,
    19–20, 27–8, 30, 32–3, 35, 43–4,
    48–51, 52–5, 56–9, 61–2
  relationship with WSC   23–4
  in South Africa   70
Churchill, Lord Randolph   1, 6–8,
    22–3, 28–9, 48
  death of   31, 228
  health issues   23, 29, 31
  letters from   24–6, 29–30
  letters to   8
  Secretary of State for India   6–7
Churchill, Sarah   85, 159
Churchill, Winston (Winston Leonard
    Spencer-Churchill, WSC)   6–7
  and animals   184, 185, 218–19
  biography, official   xvii
  birth   1
  death   32, 228
  drama, love of   18
  education   2, 4, 6, 7, 9, 14–15, 21–2
  financial issues   44–6, 47, 49, 60–2,
    136–9, 159
  flying   91–3
  marriage   84
  nature, love of   42, 44, 147

  painting   18, 109, 148, 150, 154
  political views   47–8, 49–51
  race, views on   40, 41
  and Randolph, arguments
    with   159–60
  and religion   39–41
  resignation   219–20
  self-improvement   39–40
  speech impediment   55–6
  State funeral   xvi, 228
  war correspondent   67
  watch incident   28–9
  see also health issues; literary career;
    military career; political career
Churchill College, Cambridge   224–6
Churchill War Rooms museum   176
Cockran, Bourke   36, 37
Cody, William F. (Buffalo Bill)   10
Colville, Jock   32, 197, 224, 227
Colville, Meg   227
communism   140, 215
Community Feeding Centres (British
    Restaurants)   164
Cornwallis-West, George   75, 76
Craig, James (NI Prime Minister)   135
Crete: Greek uprising in   47, 49–50
Crick, Francis   224
  letters from   225–6
Croft, Henry Page   161
  letters to   162–3
Cuba   36, 37, 48
Curzon, Lord   118, 134–5
Czechoslovakia   161

Daily Telegraph   51, 52
Dardanelles operation (Gallipoli)   102–
    3, 104, 107–8, 109
Darwin, Charles   40
Davidson, Mr   14–15, 17
de Gaulle, Charles   190–1
  letters to   191–2
de Robeck, John   103

de Souza, Louis 67
   letter to 68–9
de Valera, Éamon 181
   telegram to 182
Devonshire, 10th Duke of (Edward
   Cavendish) 184
   letters to 185
Dewar Gibb, Andrew 116
Dundee Unionist Association 133

Eden, Anthony 154–5, 218, 219–20, 221
   letters to 155–6
Edward VIII: 156
Egypt 42, 44, 206, 207
Eisenhower, Dwight 191, 192, 194,
   218
   letters to 220–1, 222–3
elections
   1906: 78
   1922: 132–3
   1945: 203
   1950: 215–17
   1956: 220–1
Elizabeth, Queen 219
European union 208–11
Everest, Elizabeth Anne (Oom) 1, 4–6
   letters to 5–6, 9–10

Fincastle, Lord 52
First World War 89–90, 94–130
   military service (WSC) 111–15
   Ploegsteert (Plug Street),
     Belgium 115–16, 127, 128
   trench warfare 111–14
   War Cabinet 134
Fisher, Jackie, Admiral 102–6, 107–8,
   119
   letters from 103–4
   letters to 105–6
Foot, Michael 215, 217
Franco, Francisco 154
Franz Ferdinand, Archduke 94

Free State of Ireland 181
French, John 111, 115
French Committee of National
   Liberation 190, 191

Gallipoli (Dardanelles operation) 102–
   3, 104, 107–8, 109
Gandhi, Mahatma 143
Garnett, Theresa 87
general strike (1926) 140–2
George VI, king 169, 178, 186
   letters from 187–8
   letters to 189
Gilbert, Martin xvii, 228
Greece 196, 212, 213, 214
Grey, Edward 88, 94, 98

Haig, Douglas 115
Halifax, Lord (Edward Wood) 169
   letters to 167
Hamilton, Ian 123
   letter to 63–6
Harmsworth, Alfred (Lord
   Northcliffe) 131
   letters to 132
Harrovian, The: letter to 21–2
Harrow School 9, 14–15, 21–2
Hawkey, James: letters to 141–2
health issues 196
   appendicitis 133
   bullet splinters 47, 48–9
   depression 108–9
   pneumonia 9, 193
   at school 4–5
   stroke 218
Hewett, Mr 43
Hitler, Adolf 145, 146, 151–2, 153,
   161, 162, 163–4, 167, 169
HMS Belfast 186
Hoare, Samuel: letters to 165–6
Hoare-Laval Pact 148, 150
Home Guard 164, 166, 177

Hopkins, Harry   179
Horne, Lord (Lord Horne of Slamannan):
    letters to   154
Howard, Lady Dorothy   81, 82, 84
Hozier, Clementine, *see* Churchill,
    Clementine (née Hozier)
hydrogen bomb   218

India   37, 39, 206, 207
    4th Hussars   37, 45, 46
    independence   7, 143, 206, 207
    WSC in   39–44, 45, 47–9, 51–5, 70
Iraq   131
Ireland   131
    Home Rule   50, 81, 88
Irish Free State   131, 135
Irish Treaty   135
iron curtain speech   203–4
Ismay, Bruce   90
Israel   206
Italy   192, 193–4

Japan   128–9, 152, 153
Jellicoe, John   106–8
    letters to   107–8
Jerome, Jennie, *see* Churchill, Lady
    Randolph
Jordan   131
journalism
    American   36–7, 38
    WSC   21, 37, 51, 52, 67–8

Kitchener, Herbert   62, 63, 64–5, 104,
    119
Knebworth House   143

Landemare, Mrs   176
Lascelles, Alan   186
League of Nations   151, 152–3
Lend-Lease Act (1941)   179
Leslie, John   12
literary career   80, 148

journalism   21, 37, 51, 52, 67–8
WORKS
    'The Dream'   32
    Great Contemporaries   145
    History of the English-Speaking
      Peoples   220
    My Early Life   4
    The River War   63
    Savrola   52, 54
    'Scaffolding of Rhetoric'   56
    The Second World War   140
    The Story of the Malakand Field
      Force   52, 56, 57
    The World Crisis   94, 128
Lloyd George, David   84–5, 88, 90,
    116, 117, 118, 123–4, 125, 127,
    132, 135–6
Longfellow, Henry Wadsworth: 'The
    Sailing of the Ship'   179
Lytton, Lord   75, 143

MacDonald, Malcolm   151
MacDonald, Ramsay   12, 148
McKenna, Mr   135–6
Maine (hospital ship)   70, 72
Malakand Field Force   51
Malta   196–7
Marlborough, 1st Duke of (John
    Churchill)   111, 148–9
Marlborough, 7th Duke of (John
    Spencer-Churchill)   1
Marlborough, 9th Duke of (Charles
    Spencer-Churchill)   34, 35, 38,
    42, 44, 75
Marrakesh, Morocco   148–50
Marsh, Eddie   106
Marshall Plan   209, 211
Martin, John   173
Masterton Smith, James   110
Menzies, Stewart ('C')   182
Mesopotamia   134
Middle East   131, 134, 222–3

Middleton, Captain 57
military career 22–4, 34, 39, 44, 48–9,
        51–5, 109–19, 124
    2nd Battalion Grenadier Guards 111
    4th Hussars 37, 45, 46
    6th Royal Scot Fusiliers 116
    21st Lancers 62–5
    Aldershot 34
    Sandhurst 23–4, 28, 56
    South African Light Horse 71
Montague Browne, Anthony 226, 227
Montague Browne, Nonie 227
Morning Post 67, 72
Morocco 148–50
Moyne, Lord 146
Munich Agreement 161
Murray, Alexander: letters to 87–9
Mussolini, Benito 148

Nasser, Gamal Abdel 221, 223
National Government 148, 151, 169
National Health Service (NHS) 215
NATO 209
Northcliffe, Lord (Alfred
        Harmsworth) 131
    letters to 132
nuclear weapons 212, 213, 218

Oliver, Vic 159
Omdurman, Battle of 62–5
Onassis, Aristotle 226

painting 18, 109, 148, 150, 152
Pakistan 206
Palestine 131, 134, 206, 208
Philip, Duke of Edinburgh 219
Plowden, Pamela 70, 75, 76,
        143
    letters to 71–4
Poland 163, 196
political career 55–9, 67, 77–80, 81,
        84–5, 119, 132–3

Chancellor of the Duchy of
        Lancaster 106
Chancellor of the Exchequer 137, 142
First Lord of the Admiralty 86–7,
        91, 94–8, 128, 163–4
Home Secretary 87, 186
Minister of Munitions 90, 100, 127–8
President of the Board of Trade 80
Prime Minister 169–75, 184–202,
        218–20
Secretary of State for the
        Colonies 131
Under-Secretary of State for the
        Colonies 80
polo 34, 35, 42, 44, 45, 58
Princip, Gavrilo 94

Ramsay, Bertram 171
    letters to 171–2
rationing 166
RMS *Titanic* 89, 90
Robertson, J. C.: letters to 133–6
Roose, Dr Robson 6, 9, 31, 32
Roosevelt, Eleanor 182
Roosevelt, Franklin 175–6, 179, 182,
        190, 191–2, 195–6
    health issues 196
    letters from 180
    letters to 183
    telegrams to 175–6, 196–7
Rota (lion) 184, 185
Rothermere, Lord 146, 147, 148–9,
        150, 151, 152, 153–4
Royal Air Force 92
Royal Naval Air Service 91, 100
Rufus II (poodle) 218–19
    letter from 219
Russia 47, 48, 128–9: *see also* Soviet
        Union

Sackville-West, Vita 155
St George's School, Ascot 2, 4, 6

Scrymgeour, Edwin 133
Second World War 89, 163–8,
    169–202
    Battle of Britain 172
    Blitz 176–7
    D-Day 186, 190
    Home Front 165–6
    Operation Dynamo 171
    Pearl Harbor 181, 182
    rationing 166
    USA and 179–81, 182–3
    War Cabinet 165, 198–9, 200
Simpson, Wallis 156
Sinclair, Archibald 116
Smith, Frederick (F. E., later Lord
    Birkenhead) 91, 118, 124–7
    letters to 125–7
Sneyd-Kynnersley, Herbert 2
Soames, Christopher 215, 217, 229
Soames, Mary 217, 228–30
    letter from 229–30
Somervell, Mr 14, 21
South Africa 67–8, 70–2
Soviet Union 163, 172, 222–3
Spain 154, 155
Spearman, Alec 213
Stalin, Joseph 195, 212
State Schools Prison, Pretoria 67
Stewart, Bimbash 72
Strom, Arne 155, 156
Sudan 62, 208
Suez Canal 221
suffrage 48, 132
    female suffrage 81–2, 86–8, 89–90,
    132
Sunny, see Marlborough, 9th Duke of
    (Charles Spencer-Churchill)

tanks 100–2
Territorial Army 163, 164

Toby (budgerigar) 218
Tory Democracy 48, 50–1
Trades Union Congress 140, 141–2,
    143
Truman, Harry S. 212
    letters from 214–15
    letters to 213
'Twelve Days' (Sackville-West) 155

Uncle, Give Us Bread (Strom) 155, 156
United Europe movement 208–11
United Nations 196, 204–5, 206,
    223
United States of America 36–8, 153
    First World War 128
    Pearl Harbor 181, 182
    Second World War 179–81, 182–3
    special relationship with 204–5,
    220, 221, 222
    WSC in 36–8, 203–4

Vanderbilt, Consuelo 37, 75
Victoria, Queen: Golden Jubilee 10–
    14

Waugh, Evelyn 159
Welldon, James 39
    letters to 40–1
West, Algy 72
West Point 36, 37–8
Western European Union 210–11
Whyte, Mr 121
Wildman-Lushington, Gilbert 91–2
Willkie, Wendell 180
Wilson, Arthur K. 103, 104
women's rights: female suffrage 81–2,
    86–8, 89–90, 132
Wood, Sir E. 64

Yalta 195–7